THE METAPHYSICAL SYSTEM OF HOBBES

THE METAPHYSICAL SYSTEM OF HOBBES

AS CONTAINED IN TWELVE CHAPTERS FROM HIS "ELEMENTS OF PHILOSOPHY CONCERNING BODY," AND IN BRIEFER EXTRACTS FROM HIS "HUMAN NATURE" AND "LEVIATHAN"

SELECTED BY

MARY WHITON CALKINS

"The world (I mean ... the whole mass of all things that are), is corporeal, that is to say, body; ... and that which is not body is no part of the universe"

GYAN

Published by

Gyan Publishing House
5, Ansari Road
Daryaganj, New Delhi-110002
Phone: 011-47034999, 9811692060
E-mail: books@gyanbooks.com

Distribution Network
gyanbooks.com
India, USA, Canada, UK, Australia, France

ISBN : 978-81-212-6370-2 (PB)
First Published, 1905

2nd Impression 2022

Printed at: Gyan Press, Delhi.

THE METAPHYSICAL SYSTEM OF HOBBES
Author: MARY WHITON CALKINS

THOMAS HOBBES
1588-1679

After a portrait by Dobson in the possession of the Royal Society

THE

Metaphysical System of Hobbes

AS CONTAINED IN TWELVE CHAPTERS FROM HIS "ELEMENTS OF PHILOSOPHY CONCERNING BODY," AND IN BRIEFER EXTRACTS FROM HIS "HUMAN NATURE" AND "LEVIATHAN"

SELECTED BY

MARY WHITON CALKINS

"The world (I mean . . the whole mass of all things that are), is corporeal, that is to say, body; . . and that which is not body is no part of the universe"

1905

PREFACE.

This condensation of the English version of Hobbes's book *Concerning Body* has been made, because the work is the completest summary of the metaphysical teaching of Hobbes and because there exists no inexpensive reprint or compendium of it. The ethical and social doctrines of Hobbes may be readily studied at first hand, by the aid of modern editions of the Leviathan or of volumes of selections from the writings of Hobbes; but for his strictly metaphysical teaching one must now have recourse to the volumes of the Molesworth edition. Teachers of modern philosophy who believe, with the writer, that the study of original texts is of incomparable value to the student must have been puzzled in their efforts to be just to the claims of materialism. Convenient expositions of idealism are readily found in the editions of Berkeley's *Principles* and *Dialogues.* But no historically important summary of materialistic doctrine has, so far, been accessible. This volume aims to supply the need and also to give an adequate impression of the *Elements of Philosophy Concerning Body.* To gain the latter end, chapters have been included from all four Parts of the work, and the headings of omitted chapters have been printed in full. To represent adequately the doctrine of Hobbes, it has been necessary to add to the formulation of materialism, as contained in the *Concerning Body,* (1) the argument for materialism, from the alleged unreality of consciousness, as it appears in chapter II. of *Human Nature;* and (2) the corollary from materialism, the teaching that spirit is a form of body, from the later chapters of Leviathan.

The only portions of this volume which duplicate recent reprints from Hobbes are chapters 1, 6, 25, and a few scattered passages from *Concerning Body,* chapter 2 of *Human Nature,* and the brief selections from *Leviathan.* The text is that of Molesworth who, save in the case of capitals and of spelling, follows the early editions. Four obvious misprints, including two misplaced Greek accents, have been changed.

The extracts from the Latin work *De Corpore,* of which *Concerning Body* is a version, are offered in recognition of the fact that Hobbes himself did not make the translation, and that the English version, spite of his revision, has not the authority of an original work. It is a pity not to reprint the Latin original, in place of the English version; but, unhappily, young American students either are not, or think that they are not, able to read Latin philosophical texts. By way of a slight protest against this form of academic illiteracy, no life of Hobbes is here printed save the autobiography, in Latin verse, written at the age of eighty-four by the vigorous old philosopher. Biographical and historical discussions will be found in the works by Robertson, Stephen and Sneath, quoted on page xxv., in the Bibliographical Note. For an exposition of the philosophy of Hobbes, all readers are referred to Hobbes himself.

M. W. C.

CONTENTS

*Only the heading of this chapter is reproduced.

*Only the heading of this chapter is reproduced.

T. HOBBES
MALMESBURIENSIS
VITA,
SCRIPTA ANNO MDCLXXII.

Birth

Natus erat noster servator Homo-Deus annos
  Mille et quingentos, octo quoque undecies.
Stabat et Hispanis in portubus inclyta classis
  Hostilis, nostro mox peritura mari:
Primo vere; dies et quintus inibat Aprilis:
  Illo vermiculus tempore nascor ego,

Birthplace

In Malmesburia; baptisma a patre ministro
  Accepi, et nomen mi dedit ille suum.
Oppidulum parvum est, habuit sed multa relatu
  Digna, atque imprimis cœnobium celebre,
Et castrum, melius nisi sint duo castra vocanda,
  Colle sita, et bino flumine cincta fere.
Concilium regni binis burgensibus auget;
  Nunc quoque priscus honor permanet ille loci.
Hic et Athelstani conduntur nobilis ossa,
  Atque super tumulum saxeus ipse jacet.
Præmia virtutis populo dedit ille, propinquos
  Sanguine Danorum qui madefecit agros:

Study

Huc et ab Aldhelmo deducta est musa Latina,
  Hic habuit primam lingua Latina scholam.
Non est ut patriæ pudeat; sed tempus iniquum
  Conqueror, et mecum tot quoque nata mala.
Fama ferebat enim diffusa per oppida nostra,
  Extremum genti classe venire diem.
Atque metum tantum concepit tunc mea mater,
  Ut pareret geminos, meque metumque simul.
Hinc est, ut credo, patrios quod abominor hostes,
  Pacem amo cum musis, et faciles socios.
Disco loqui quatuor, totidem legere, et numerare,
  Non bene præterea fingere literulas.

Oxford

Sex annis ad verba steti Græcæ atque Latinæ,
Et decimo quarto mittor ad Oxonium.
Huc Magdalenæ veniens admittor in aulam,
Inque ima logicæ classe locatus eram.
Et prælectori cum primis sedulus adsum;
Is licet imberbis cum gravitate legit,
Barbara, celarent, darii, ferio, baralypton,
Hos, dicebat, habet prima figura modos.
Cæsare, camestres, festino, baroco, darapti,
Hæc etiam totidem stat variata modis.
Felapton, disamis, datisi, bocardo, ferison,
Sunt rursus totidem legitimique modi.
Quos tarde disco, disco tamen, abjicioque,
Admittorque meo quæque probare modo.
Admoveor physicæ, conflataque cuncta magister
Materia et forma, ut partibus, esse docet;
Et species rerum, volitando per æra, formas
Donare hinc oculis, auribus inde sonos.
Multos effectus tribuit *syn et antipathiæ,*
Et supra captum talia multa meum.
Ergo ad amœna magis me verto, librosque revolvo,
Queis prius instructus, non bene doctus eram.
Pascebamque animum chartis imitantibus orbem,
Telluris faciem, et sydera picta videns:
Gaudebam soli comes ire, et cernere cunctis
Terricolis ustos qua facit arte dies.
Quoque Dracus filo Neptunum, Candisiusque
Cinxerunt medium; quæque adiere loca·
Atque hominum exiguos, si possem, cernere nidos,
Et picta ignotis monstra videre locis.
Tempore sed justo cum Baccalaureus Artis
Essem (namque hic est primus in arte gradus)

Service of Duke of Devonshire

Oxonium linquo, servitum me fero in amplam
Gentis Candisiæ conspicuamque domum;
Rectorisque aulæ commendat Epistola nostræ:
Accipior, placita conditione steti:

Atque adolescenti mox applicor ipse adolscens:
Tunc patris imperio subditus ille fuit.
Huic ego servivi bis denos gnaviter annos;
Non Dominus tantum, verum et amicus erat.
Pars erat illa meæ multo dulcissima vitæ,
Et nunc sæpe mihi somnia grata facit.
Ille per hoc tempus mihi præbuit otia, libros
Omnimodos studiis præbuit ille meis.
Study of classics
Vertor ego ad nostras, ad Græcas, atque Latinas
Historias; etiam carmina sæpe lego.
Flaccus, Virgilius, fuit et mihi notus Homerus,
Euripides, Sophocles, Plautus, Aristophanes,
Pluresque; et multi Scriptores Historiarum:
Sed mihi præ reliquis Thucydides placuit.
Is Democratia ostendit mihi quam sit inepta,
Et quantum cœtu plus sapit unus homo.
Hunc ego scriptorem verti, qui diceret Anglis,
Consultaturi rhetoras ut fugerent.
Travel
Urbes externas eadem per tempora vidi,
Germanas, Francas, Ausoniasque adii.
Mox Dominum morbo devictum vita reliquit,
Extremo (ut credas) sed reditura die.
Ante tamen fecit mihi ne servire necesse
Esset, qui modice vivere suetus eram.
Deinde domo placita nimium neglectus abivi,
Parisiisque moror mensibus octodecim.
Inde mei Domini revocor præceptor ut essem
Nato; Devoniæ tunc Comes ille fuit.
Hunc Romanarum sensus cognoscere vocum;
Jungere quoque decet verba Latina modo;
Fallere quaque solent indoctos rhetores arte;
Quid facit orator, quidque poeta facit;
Et demonstrandi docui præcepta, globique
Mundani faciem, multiplicesque gyros.
Litibus et finem, faciunt quas *plus*, *minus*, et *par*,
Qua posset usta ponere lege dedi.
Hæs illum docui per septem sedulos annos;
Ille celer didicit, retinuitque memor.

Nec tamen hoc tempus libris consumpsimus omne,
Ni mundum libri dixeris esse loco.

Second journey

Italiæ multas, Gallorum et vidimus urbes;
Secessus dulces vidimus Allobrogum.
Ast ego perpetuo naturam cogito rerum,
Seu rate, seu curru, sive ferebar equo.
Et mihi visa quidem est toto res unica mundo
Vera, licet multis falsificata modis:
Unica vera quidem, sed quæ sit basis earum
Rerum, quas falso dicimus esse aliquid;
Qualia somnus habet fugitiva, et qualia vitris
Arbitrio possum multiplicare meo;
Phantasiæ, nostri soboles cerebri, nihil extra;
Partibus internis nil nisi motus inest.

Study of physics

Hinc est quod, physicam quisquis vult discere, motus
Quid possit, debet perdidicisse prius.
Ergo materiæ motusque arcana recludo;
Sic tempus vacuum fallo per Italiam.
Scribo nihil, facio adversaria nulla, magistra
Quæ docuit, præsens nam mihi semper erat.
Linquimus Italiam, rursusque redimus ad alta
Mœnia Lutetiæ, tectaque magnifica.
Hic ego Mersennum novi, communico et illi
De rerum motu quæ meditatus eram.
Is probat, et multis commendat; tempore ab illo
Inter philosophos et numerabar ego.

Study of philosophy and psychology

In patriam rursus post menses octo reversus,
De conectendis cogito notitiis.
Motibus a variis feror ad rerum variarum
Dissimiles species, materiæque dolos;
Motusque internos hominum, cordisque latebras;
Denique ad imperii justitiæque bona.
His ego me mersi studiis. Nam philosophandi
Corpus, Homo, Civis continet omne genus.
Tres super his rebus statuo conscribere libros;

Materiemque mihi congero quoque die.
Nascitur interea scelus execrabile belli,
Et veniunt studiis tempora iniqua meis.
Sexcentesimus et jam quadragesimus annus
Post millesimum erat virginis a puero,
Cum patriam invasit morbus mirabilis, unde
Innumeri e doctis post periere viri.
Quo quicunque fuit tactus, divina putabat
Atque humana uni cognita jura sibi.
Jamque in procinctu bellum stetit. Horreo spectans;
Meque ad dilectam confero Lutetiam.
De Cive Postque duos annos edo *De Cive* libellum,
Qui placuit doctis, et novus omnis erat;
Versus et in varias linguas cum laude legebar,
Gentibus et late nomine notus eram.
Laudabat mediis in Erynnibus Anglia, et illi
Quorum consiliis cognitus hostis eram
Sed quod consiliis præsentibus utile non est,
Quantumvis justum, quis putat esse bonum?
De Corpore Inde annis quatuor libri *De Corpore* forman,
Qua sit scribendus, nocte dieque puto.
Comparo corporeas moles; et cogito rerum
Visarum formas quid variare potest.
Quæro quibus possim rationis Protea vinclis
Stringere, fassurum qua tegit arte dolos.
Adfuit e Minimis Mersennus, fidus amicus;
Vir doctus, sapiens, eximieque bonus.
Cujus cella scholis erat omnibus anterferenda;
Professorum omnes ambitione tument.
Illi portabat, si dignum forte porisma
Reppererat quisquam, principiumve novum.
Perspicuo et proprio sermone, carente figuris
Rhetoricis, gnomis, ambitione, dolo,
Ille dedit doctis, qui vellent, rursus ut illud
Vel statim possent, vel trutinare domi.
Edidit e multisque inventis optima quæque;
Signans authoris nomine quidque sui.
Circa Mersennum convertebatur ut axem
Unumquodque artis sidus in orbe suo.

Sævierat bellum quatuor civile per annos,
Anglos, Hibernos triverat atque Scotos.
Perfidaque in castris mansit Fortuna scelestis:
Diffugere via qua potuere probi.
Ipse hæres regni Carolus, comitante caterva
Armis clarorum et nobilitate virum,
Lutetiam venit, expectans dum tempora iniqua
Transirent, populi desineretque furor.
Tunc ego decreram *De Corpore* scribere librum,
Cujus materies tota parata fuit.
Sed cogor differre; *pati tot tantaque fœda*
Apponi jussis crimina, nolo, Dei.
Divinas statuo quam primum absolvere leges;
Idque ago paulatim, sollicitusque diu.
Namque mathematicæ studiis dum Principi adessem,
Non potui studiis semper adesse meis.
Dein per sex menses morbo decumbo, propinquæ
Accinctus morti; nec fugio, illa fugit.
Leviathan Perfeci librum patrio sermone; ut ab Anglis
Posset sæpe meis, utiliterque legi:
Londinoque typis celer evolat in regiones
Vicinas, notus nomine *Leviathan.*
Militat ille liber nunc regibus omnibus, et qui
Nomine sub quovis regia ura tenent.
Interea regem vendit Scotus, et necat Anglus;
Jus regni Carolus jamque Secundus habet,
Lutetiæ residens. Vim regni turba rebellis
Occupat, et populum jam sine lege regit,
Et nomen (quamvis pauci) sibi Parliamenti
Sumens, se satiat sanguine nobilium;
Dejiciunt mitras, nec firmant Presbyteratum;
Clerica nil illic profuit ambitio.
Exile Lutetiam ad regem multus venit inde scholaris
Expulsus patria, tristis, egenus, onus.
Huc fuit usque meis studiis pax, multiplicata
Dum facerent annos octo per octo meos;
Sed meus ille liber, simul atque scholaribus illis
Lectus erat, Jani dissiluere fores.

Nam Regi accusor falso, quasi facta probarem
 Impia Cromwelli, jus scelerique darem.
Creditur; adversis in partibus esse videbar;
 Perpetuo jubeor Regis abesse domo.
Tunc venit in mentem mihi Dorislaus,* et Ascham;*
 Tanquam proscripto terror ubique aderat.
Nec de rege queri licuit. *Nam tunc adolescens*
 Credidit ille, quibus credidit ante pater.
Return In patriam redeo tutelæ non bene certus,
 Sed nullo potui tutior esse loco:
Frigus erat, nix alta, senex ego, ventus acerbus;
 Vexat equus sternax et salebrosa via.
Londinum veniens, ne clam venisse viderer,
 Concilio Status conciliandus eram.
Quo facto, statim summa cum pace recedo,
 Et sic me studiis applico, ut ante, meis.
Solum regnabat tunc nomine *Parliamentum;*
 Præsul erat nullus, Presbyterusque nihil.
Omnia miles erat, committier omnia et uni
 Poscebat; tacite Cromwell is unus erat.
Regia conanti calamo defendere jura,
 Quis vitio vertat regia jura petens?
Scribere cuique fuit libertas, quod sibi visum
 Esset, contento vivere more loci.
Leviathan clerum at totum mihi fecerat hostem;
 Hostis Theologum nidus uterque fuit.
Nam dum Papalis Regni contrecto tumorem,
 Hos, licet abscissos, lædere visus eram.
Contra *Leviathan,* primo, convicia scribunt,
 Et causa, ut tanto plus legeretur, erant.
Firmius inde stetit, spero stabitque per omne
 Ævum, defensus viribus ipse suis.
Justitiæ mensura, atque ambitionis elenchus,
 Regum arx, pax populo, si doceatur, erit.

---

* Regicidæ infames; quorum hic apud Hispanos, ille apud Fœderatos Belgas a Parliamentariis legatus, a regiis confossi perierunt.

Ante duos minima præmisi mole libellos;
Sed nec inest parvis gratia parva libris.
Ille* docet motus animi et phantasmata sensus,
Nec sanos patitur spectra timere viros:
Alter† at Imperii sanctissima jura repandit,
Quæque rudes populos vincula sacra tenent.
Tandem etiam absolvo librum *De Corpore,* cujus
Materies simul et forma geometrica est.

Controversy on mathematics

Tunc venit in lucem, tota plaudente caterva
Algebristarum, Wallisii algebrica,
Illa Geometriæ pestis, quæ cœperat ante
Annos plus centum, nunc et ubique furit.
Ars fuerat numeros quæsitos inveniendi,
Quam docuit Cheber, et quam Diophantus habet.
Deinde per hanc artem solam problemata solvi
Posse geometriæ cuncta Vieta docet.
Addidit Oxoniæ Prælector Savilianus
Wallisius multo nobile dogma magis:
Nempe infinitæ molis finem esse, et habere
Finitum partes et sine fine datas:
Quæ duo fecerunt insanos dogmata, quotquot
Festinaverunt esse geometrici.
Hæc mihi causa satis scribendi est justa libelli,
(Annos natus eram septuaginta duos)

Six lessons

In quo, Colloquiis ego Sex non molliter istos
Tango geometras, ut meruere, novos;
Sed nil profeci, magnis authoribus error
Fultus erat; cessit sic medicina malo.
Tunc quoque scribo duos patrio sermone libellos
Contra Bramhallum. Quæstio sola fuit,
Cujus ad arbitrium volumus, nostrumne, Deine:
Ille scholam sequitur, sed mihi dux ratio est.

Problems

Sex quoque post paulo scripsi Problemata, librum
Exiguum, at puræ fonticulum physicæ.

---

* Liber *de Natura Humana.*
† Lib. *de Corpore Politico.*

Nam doceo natura locis qua dejicit arte
  Sublimes lapides, res aliasque graves;
Qua situla sol haurit aquas; ut frigora ventus
  Efficit; et venti qua ratione volant:
Quo pendent steriles, volitantque per æra nubes,
  Quo fulcro gravidæ destituente ruunt;
Et quo consistunt durorum glutine partes,
  Duraque quæ rursus mollia causa facit;
Unde fragor cœlo, qua nix glaciesque fit arte;
  Excussusque altis emicat ignis aquis;
Quid res exiguas conjungit in ære sparsas,
  Et calidum Phœbus qua ratione facit;
Herculeusque lapis ferrum quibus attrahit uncis,
  Observatque suæ matris utrumque polum;
Cur mare non æquis ad littora volvitur undis;
  Anno, mense, die quoque, bis auget aquas;
Et quare, vento duce, navis it obvia vento;
  Hæc habet et monstrat parvulus ille liber.
Et valitura puto cum tempore; quandoquidem nunc
  Inter tot Momos irreprehensa manent.
Æris et parvo naturam scribo libello
  Adversus quandam machinam inanificam.
Tunc physicam linquens, ad amata mathemata vertor;
  Namque meo tandem cesserat hostis agro.
Tantum non lapidem potuissem vera docere,
  Clamosas speret nemo docere scholas.
De Principiis At *De Principiis* alium tamen edo libellum,
  Fecique ut posset clarius esse nihil.
In quo naturam rationis ita explico, ut illam
  Nemo non claram diceret atque probam.
Hac mihi parte fuit victoria cognita cunctis,
  Dissimulant aliis vulnera magna locis;
Deficiunt animis, sed deficientibus insto,
  Culminaque inscendo summa geometriæ.
Namque parem cyclum quadrato publico; necnon
  Jactatum Pythii monstro porisma Dei;

Demonstrata prius, sed non rationibus iisdem,
  Sperabam methodo vincere posse nova.
Sed nil profeci, densis umbonibus obstant,
  Cedere quos puduit, semi-mathematici.
Ergo meam statuo non ultra perdere opellam,
  Indocile expectans discere posse pecus.
Rosetum, Deinde librum scribo, quem nomine dico *Rosetum,*
  Præcipuo densum flore geometriæ.
Wallisius contra pugnat; victusque videbar
  Algebristarum Theologumque scholis.
Et simul eductus castris exercitus omnis
  Pugnæ securus Wallisianus ovat;
Quem cum vidissem salebroso insistere campo,
  Stabat ubi radix densa, molesta, tenax,
Pugna placet, vertor; numerum licet infinitum
  Temporis in puncto dissipo, sterno, fugo.
Bella mea audisti. Quid vis tibi dicier ultra?
  An quam dives, id est, quam sapiens fuerim?
Anne refert quot agros habui, quot millia nummum?
  Si percontator forte rogabit et hoc,
Exiguus mihi fundus erat propriusque relictus
  Quem fratri dono, ductus amore, dedi.
Parva superficies, sed millia multa ferebat
  Granorum tritici, nam bona terra fuit.
Longa satis votis regum; et nisi tota deorsum
  Tensa foret, Rex nunc magnus haberer ego.
Ut primum belli sensi civilis odorem,
  Et populum ventos vidi agitasse levem:
Quæro locum studiis, et vitæ commodiorem,
  Hinc me Parisios transfero remque meam.
Quingentæ mihi erat numerata pecunia libræ,
  Cum fugiens patriæ littora linquo meæ:
Legacy His aliæ paulo post accessere ducentæ.*
  Et simul immensus perpetuusque dolor.
(Godolphine jaces; puræ rationis amator,
  Justitiæ et Veri miles amande, vale.)

---

* Ex Legato Sydn. Godolphini.

Venit et e patria mihi pensio certa quotannis,
  Bis* quadragintis constitit illa libris.
Pension from King Deinde redux mihi Rex concessit habere quotannis
  Centum alias libras ipsius ex loculis,
Dulce mihi donum. Convicia sperno aliorum,
  Quando teste ipso judicor esse probus.
His ego contentus vivo, nec præfero plura;
  Quis vellet sanus re minor esse sua?
Rem, si quando lubet, per vestros supputo *Sousos,*
  Ut fiat major: si neque sic satis est,
Per *Maravedisios* numero, videorque beatus
  Crœsos et Crassos vincere divitiis.
Ipse meos nosti, Verdusi candide, mores,
  Et tecum cuncti qui mea scripta legunt.
Nam mea vita meis non est incongrua scriptis:
  Justitiam doceo, justitiamque colo.
Improbus esse potest nemo qui non sit avarus,
  Nec pulchrum quisquam fecit avarus opus.
Octoginta ego jam complevi et quatuor annos:
  Pene acta est vitæ fabula longa meæ.

* Ex munere Comitis Devoniæ.

TOPICAL LIST OF THE WRITINGS OF HOBBES.

The dates and the Latin titles are transferred from the catalogue of Ant. à Wood, as reprinted in Molesworth's edition of the *Opera Latina* (cited as *Op. Lat.*), Vol. I. The English titles are those of Molesworth's edition of the English works (cited as *E. W.*), except when these conflict with the titles quoted by Robertson from the early editions. All works, unless otherwise indicated, were published in London.

I. Writings on Metaphysics.

1641. Objections in Cartesii de prima Philosophia Meditationes.

Published in all the early editions of Descartes's Meditations, Paris and Amsterdam.

1655. Elementa Philosophiæ Sectio prima de Corpore, 8vo, 1655. *Op. Lat. Vol. I.*

1656. Elements of Philosophy, The First Section Concerning Body. *E. W. I.*

A translation, not by Hobbes, of the *De Corpore.* Cf. pp. ii. and 183 of this volume.

See, also, for metaphysical discussion, *Leviathan* (esp. chapters 12, 31, 34); the ethical writings; An Answer to a Book . . . by Dr. Bramhall.

II. Writings on Mathematics and Physics.

1644. Tractatus Opticus. *Op. Lat. V.*

Published by Mersenne, in 1644, in his *Cogitata Physico-Mathematica.*

1655. De Corpore.

1656. Concerning Body.

These two works, already quoted by their full titles, contain the mathematical as well as the metaphysical doctrine of Hobbes. This follows naturally from his conviction, that "every part of the universe is body," for, if this be granted, the mathematical laws of the physical world are the principles of all reality. Hobbes, however, despite his pretensions, was never other than an amateur in mathematics; and the mathematical chapters of *De Corpore*, along with much irrelevant matter, contain one colossal blunder: the attempt (C. XX.) at squaring the circle. The error was exposed at once by Wallis, Savilian professor of geometry at Oxford, in his *Elenchus Geometriæ Hobbionæ*. This work was the starting-point of a bitter controversy, lasting more than twenty years. So far as the mathematical issues were concerned, Hobbes was always in the wrong; but he never acknowledged defeat, and returned with courage worthy of a better cause, again and again to the unequal struggle. (Cf. esp. Robertson's "Hobbes," pp. 167 *seq.*) It should, however, be noted that he modified the mathematical chapters, both in the later editions of *De Corpore* (followed in Molesworth's *Op. Lat.*, which are based on the collected edition of 1668) and also in the English version, *Concerning Body*. All the titles in this section are of works concerned in this discussion. Unless otherwise described, all are to be found either in *Op. Lat. IV.* or in *E. W. VII.*

1656. Six Lessons to the Professors of the Mathematics, . . . in the Chairs set up by . . . Sir Henry Savile in the University of Oxford.

1657. ΣΤΙΓΜΑΙ or Marks of the Absurd Geometry, Rural Language, Scottish Church Politics and Barbarisms of John Wallis.

1660. Examinatio et Emendatio Mathematicæ Hodiernæ.

1661. Dialogus Physicus, sive de Natura Æris.

1661. De Duplicatione Cubi, Paris.

Molesworth does not print this in the original French, but only in the modified English form, as the concluding pages of the Dialogus Physicus.

1662. Problemata Physica, una cum Magnitudine Circuli.

1666. De Principiis et Ratiocinatione Geometrarum.

1669. Quadratura Circuli, Cubatio Sphæræ, Duplicatio Cubi; una cum Responsione ad Objectiones Geometriæ Professoris Saviliani.

1671. Rosetum Geometricum, . . . cum Censura brevi Doctrinæ Wallisianæ de Motu. *Op. Lat V.*

1671. Three Papers Presented to the Royal Society against Dr. Wallis.

1672. Lux Mathematica. *Op. Lat. V.*

1672. Principia et Problemata aliquot geometrica ante desperata . . . *Op. Lat. V.*

1678. Decameron Physiologicum, or Ten Dialogues of Natural Philosophy.

(POSTHUMOUS WORKS.)

1682. Seven Philosophical Problems and Two Propositions of Geometry.

A shortened translation of *Problemata Physica,* 1662.

III. Writings on Psychology.

1650. Human Nature. *E. W. IV.*

The logical foundation both of Hobbes's metaphysics and of his political philosophy. Actually the first of his systematic works, written in 1640 and at that time combined with the *De Corpore Politico,* under the title, *The Elements of Law, Natural and Politique.* (Cf. Robertson, "Hobbes," p. 51 and p. 67, Note.)

1657. De Homine, sive Elementorum Philosophiæ Sectio Secunda. *Op. Lat. II.*

An ill proportioned work, less complete than *Human Nature* and containing many, chiefly irrelevant, chapters on optics.

See also, for psychological discussion: *Leviathan*, Pt. I.; *De Corpore*, Pt. IV.; *Concerning Body*, Pt. IV.; *Decameron Physiologicum*.

IV. Writings on "Civil Philosophy (or Politics)."

1642. Elementorum Philosophiæ Sectio Tertia De Cive. Paris.

Privately printed. Re-printed, in 1647, with altered title, thus:

1647. Elementa Philosophica de Cive. Amsterdam. *Op. Lat. II.*

1651. Philosophical Rudiments concerning Government and Society. *E. W. II.*

1650. De Corpore Politico, or the Elements of Law, Moral and Politic. *E. W. IV.*

Written in 1640 (Cf. Note, above, on *Human Nature.*) As compared with the *De Cive*, this work lays less emphasis on the power of the state in ecclesiastical matters.

1651. Leviathan: Or, the Matter, Form and Power of a Commonwealth, Ecclesiastical and Civil. *E. W. III.*

The most popular, forcible and detailed discussion of the political theory of Hobbes, prefixed by several chapters on psychology.

1668. Leviathan. Amsterdam. *Op. Lat. III.*

A translation, by Hobbes himself, into Latin. The Latin version omits and alters certain portions of the English original. It included:

1668. Appendix ad Leviathan. Amsterdam. *Op. Lat. III.*

The Appendix sets forth (1) that the teaching of *Leviathan* is not heretical and (2) that there remains in England no court of heresy.

(POSTHUMOUS WORKS.)

For the following works, Hobbes did not succeed in obtaining the censor's license: —

1680. Behemoth: The History of the Causes of the Civil Wars of England . . . from the Year 1640 to the Year 1660. *E. W. VI.*

Written about 1668. Several unauthorized and inaccurate editions appeared before 1680.

1680. An Historical Narration concerning Heresy and the Punishment Thereof. (London?) *E. W. IV.*

Written about 1666, after the abortive parliamentary proceedings against *Leviathan.*

1681. A Dialogue between a Philosopher and a Student of the Common Laws of England. *E. W. VI.*

Written about 1666.

1682. An Answer to a Book Published by Dr. Bramhall . . . called *Catching of the Leviathan. E. W. IV.*

Written in 1668. A refutation of Bramhall's charge, "that the Hobbian principles are destructive to Christianity and to all religion."

1688. Historia Ecclesiastica Romana, Poema . . . ubi de Superstitionis Origine, progressu, &c. *Op. Lat. V.*

Written, about 1670. An English version was published in 1722.

V. Writings on Ethics.

1654. Of Liberty and Necessity. *E. W. IV.*

Written in in 1646, as part of a private discussion with Bishop Bramhall; published without the consent of Hobbes. (Cf. Robertson, "Hobbes," p. 163 *seq.*)

1656. The Questions concerning Liberty, Necessity and Chance, Clearly Stated and Debated between Dr. Bramhall, Bishop of Derry, and Thomas Hobbes, of Malmesbury. *E. W. V.*

See, also, Writings on Civil Philosophy.

VI. Writings on Rhetoric and on Miscellaneous Subjects.

1636. De Mirabilibus Pecci liber.

Account of an excursion round Derbyshire Peak. Written before 1628, *Op. Lat. V.*

1650. The Answer of Mr. Hobbes to Sir William Davenant's Preface before Gondibert.

A letter on the nature of poetry, apropos of the poet laureate's heroic poem, *Gondibert, E. W. IV.*

1669. Letter to the Right Honorable Edw. Howard.

Published as prefix to Mr. Howard's poem, *The British Princes.*

(posthumous works.)

1681. The Whole Art of Rhetoric. *E. W. VI.*

An English abstract of that Latin version of Aristotle's Rhetoric, dictated between 1630 and 1640, by Hobbes, to his pupil, the young Earl of Devonshire. To this is added, in the edition of 1681, short treatises on:

The Art of Rhetoric,

The Art of Sophistry.

VII. Translations.

1628. Eight Books of the Peloponnesian War, written by Thucydides . . . Interpreted with Faith and Diligence immediately out of the Greek. *E. W. VIII. and IX.*

1674. Voyage of Ulysses.

A rhymed translation of Odyssey, Bks. IX.-XII., later incorporated in the complete translation:

1675. The Iliads and Odysses of Homer. Translated out of Greek into English. With a large preface concerning the Virtues of an Heroic Poem. *E. W. X.*

VIII. Personal Writings.

1662. Considerations upon the Reputation, Loyalty, Manners and Religion of Thomas Hobbes. *E. W. IV.*

A reply to the personal charges of Wallis's *Hobbius Heautontimorumenos.*

1674. Epistola ad Antony à Wood. (London?) Not included in *Op. Lat.*

A protest against Dean Fell's abuse of Hobbes in the translation of Wood's *History and Antiquities of Oxford.*

1679. Vita Ejus Latino Carmine. *Op. Lat. I.*

(POSTHUMOUS WORKS.)

1681. T. Hobbes Malmesburiensis Vita. *Op. Lat. I.*

A prose life, attributed to Hobbes.

See, also, for personal allusions, all the controversial writings of Hobbes; and for a few letters, *E. W. VII.* and *Op. Lat. V.*

BIBLIOGRAPHICAL NOTE.

For references to contemporary criticism of Hobbes, usually unsympathetic and often violent, see R. Blackbourne, Vitæ Hobbianæ Auctarium (1681), *Op. Lat. I., p. lxix. seq.*

For references to works of exposition and of criticism, from the later seventeenth century onward, see Sneath, "The Ethics of Hobbes" (1898), Introduction, p. xii. *seq.;* Robertson, (1) "Hobbes" (1886), chaps. IX. and X., (2) article in Encycl. Brit., 9th ed., vol. XII., footnotes.

The most useful of recent works on the life, writing and system of Hobbes include the books, just mentioned, of Robertson and of Sneath, and the following: "Hobbes" (1904), by Leslie Stephen, and "Hobbes, Leben und Lehre," (Stuttgart, 1896) by F. Tönnies, and Woodbridge, "The Philosophy of Hobbes in Extracts and Notes from his Writings" (1903).

ELEMENTS OF PHILOSOPHY.

THE FIRST SECTION,

CONCERNING BODY,

WRITTEN IN LATIN

BY

THOMAS HOBBES OF MALMESBURY,

AND

TRANSLATED INTO ENGLISH.

THE

TRANSLATOR TO THE READER.

IF, when I had finished my translation of this first section of the Elements of Philosophy, I had presently committed the same to the press, it might have come to your hands sooner than now it doth. But as I undertook it with much diffidence of my own ability to perform it well; so I thought fit, before I published it, to pray Mr. Hobbes to view, correct, and order it according to his own mind and pleasure. Wherefore, though you find some places enlarged, others altered, and two chapters, XIII and XX, almost wholly changed, you may nevertheless remain assured, that as now I present it to you, it doth not at all vary from the author's own sense and meaning. * * * * * * * * * *

THE

AUTHOR'S EPISTLE TO THE READER.

THINK not, Courteous Reader, that the philosophy, the elements whereof I am going to set in order, is that which makes philosophers' stones, nor that which is found in the metaphysic codes; but that it is the natural reason of man, busily flying up and down among the creatures, and bringing back a true report of their order, causes and effects. Philosophy, therefore, the child of the world and your own mind, is within yourself; perhaps not fashioned yet, but like the world its father, as it was in the beginning, a thing confused. Do, therefore, as the statuaries do, who, by hewing off that which is superfluous, do not make but find the image. Or imitate the creation: if you will be a philosopher in good earnest, let your reason move upon the deep of your own cogitations and experience; those things that lie in confusion must be set asunder, distinguished, and every one stamped with its own name set in order; that is to say, your method must resemble that of the creation. The order of the creation was, *light, distinction of day and night,* the *firmament,* the *luminaries, sensible creatures, man;* and, after the creation, the *commandment.* Therefore the order of contemplation will be, *reason, definition, space,* the *stars, sensible quality, man;* and after man is grown up, *subjection to command.* In the first part of this section, which is entitled Logic, I set up the light of reason. In the second, which hath for title the Grounds of

Philosophy, I distinguish the most common notions by accurate definition, for the avoiding of confusion and obscurity. The third part concerns the expansion of space, that is Geometry. The fourth contains the Motion of the Stars, together with the doctrine of sensible qualities.

In the second section, if it please God, shall be handled *Man*. In the third section, the doctrine of *Subjection* is handled already. This is the method I followed; and if it like you, you may use the same; for I do but propound, not commend to you anything of mine. But whatsoever shall be the method you will like, I would very fain commend philosophy to you, that is to say, the study of wisdom, for want of which we have all suffered much damage lately. For even they, that study wealth, do it out of love to wisdom; for their treasures serve them but for a looking-glass, wherein to behold and contemplate their own wisdom. Nor do they, that love to be employed in public business, aim at anything but place wherein to show their wisdom. Neither do voluptuous men neglect philosophy, but only because they know not how great a pleasure it is to the mind of man to be ravished in the vigorous and perpetual embraces of the most beauteous world. Lastly, though for nothing else, yet because the mind of man is no less impatient of empty time than nature is of empty place, to the end you be not forced for want of what to do, to be troublesome to men that have business, or take hurt by falling into idle company, but have somewhat of your own wherewith to fill up your time, I recommend unto you to study philosophy. Farewell.

T. H.

COMPUTATION OR LOGIC.

CHAPTER I.

OF PHILOSOPHY.

1. The Introduction.—2. The Definition of Philosophy explained.—3. Ratiocination of the Mind.—4. Properties, what they are.—5. How Properties are known by Generation, and contrarily.—6. The Scope of Philosophy.—7. The Utility of it.—8. The Subject.—9. The Parts of it.—10. The Epilogue.

PHILOSOPHY seems to me to be amongst men now, in the same manner as corn and wine are said to have been in the world in ancient time. For from the beginning there were vines and ears of corn growing here and there in the fields; but no care was taken for the planting and sowing of them. Men lived therefore upon acorns; or if any were so bold as to venture upon the eating of those unknown and doubtful fruits, they did it with danger of their health. In like manner, every man brought Philosophy, that is, Natural Reason, into the world with him; for all men can reason to some degree, and concerning some things: but where there is need of a long series of reasons, there most men wander out of the way, and fall into error for want of method, as it were for want of sowing and planting, that is, of improving their reason. And from hence it comes to pass, that they who content themselves with daily experience, which may be likened to feeding upon acorns, and either reject, or not much regard philosophy, are commonly esteemed, and are, indeed, men of sounder judgment than those who, from opinions, though not vulgar, yet full of uncertainty, and carelessly received, do nothing but dispute and wrangle, like men that are not well in their wits. I confess, indeed, that that part of philosophy by which magnitudes and figures are computed, is highly improved. But because I have not observed the like advancement in the other parts of it, my purpose is, as far forth as I am able, to lay open the few and first Elements of Philosophy in general, as so many seeds from which pure and true Philosophy may hereafter spring up by little and little.

I am not ignorant how hard a thing it is to weed out of men's minds such inveterate opinions as have taken root there, and been confirmed in them by the authority of most eloquent writers; especially seeing true (that is, accurate) Philosophy professedly rejects not only the paint and false colours of language, but even the very ornaments and graces of the same; and the first grounds of all science are not only not beautiful, but poor, arid, and, in appearance, deformed. Nevertheless, there being certainly some men, though but few, who are delighted with truth and strength of reason in all things, I thought I might do well to take this pains for the sake even of those few. I proceed therefore to the matter, and take my beginning from the very definition of philosophy, which is this.

2. PHILOSOPHY *is such knowledge of effects or appearances, as we acquire by true ratiocination from the knowledge we have first of their causes or generation: And again, of such causes or generations as may be from knowing first their effects.*

For the better understanding of which definition, we must consider, first, that although Sense and Memory of things, which are common to man and all living creatures, be knowledge, yet because they are given us immediately by nature, and not gotten by ratiocination, they are not philosophy.

Secondly, seeing Experience is nothing but memory; and Prudence, or prospect into the future time, nothing but expectation of such things as we have already had experience of, Prudence also is not to be esteemed philosophy.

BY RATIOCINATION, I mean *computation.* Now to compute, is either to collect the sum of many things that are added together, or to know what remains when one thing is taken out of another. *Ratiocination,* therefore, is the same with *addition* and *substraction;* and if any man add *multiplication* and *division,* I will not be against it, seeing multiplication is nothing but addition of equals one to another, and division nothing but a substraction of equals one from another, as often as is possible. So that all ratiocination is comprehended in these two operations of the mind, addition and substraction.

3. But how by the *ratiocination* of our mind, we add and substract in our silent thoughts, without the use of words, it will be necessary for me to make intelligible by an example or two. If therefore a man see something afar off and obscurely, although no appellation had yet been given to anything, he will, notwithstanding, have the same idea of that thing for which now, by imposing a name on it, we call it *body.* Again, when, by coming nearer, he sees the same thing thus and thus, now in one place and now in another, he will have a new idea thereof, namely, that for which

we now call such a thing *animated.* Thirdly, when standing nearer, he perceives the figure, hears the voice, and sees other things which are signs of a rational mind, he has a third idea, though it have yet no appellation, namely, that for which we now call anything *rational.* Lastly, when, by looking fully and distinctly upon it, he conceives all that he has seen as one thing, the idea he has now is compounded of his former ideas, which are put together in the mind in the same order in which these three single names, *body, animated, rational,* are in speech compounded into this one name, *body-animated-rational,* or *man.* In like manner, of the several conceptions of *four sides, equality of sides, and right angles,* is compounded the conception of a *square.* For the mind may conceive a figure of four sides without any conception of their equality, and of that equality without conceiving a right angle; and may join together all these single conceptions into one conception or one idea of a square. And thus we see how the conceptions of the mind are compounded. Again, whosoever sees a man standing near him, conceives the whole idea of that man; and if, as he goes away, he follow him with his eyes only, he will lose the idea of those things which were signs of his being rational, whilst, nevertheless, the idea of a body-animated remains still before his eyes, so that the idea of rational is subtracted from the whole idea of man, that is to say, of body-animated-rational, and there remains that of body-animated; and a while after, at a greater distance, the idea of animated will be lost, and that of body only will remain; so that at last, when nothing at all can be seen, the whole idea will vanish out of sight. By which examples, I think, it is manifest enough what is the internal ratiocination of the mind without words.

We must not therefore think that computation, that is, ratiocination, has place only in numbers, as if man were distinguished from other living creatures (which is said to have been the opinion of *Pythagoras*) by nothing but the faculty of numbering; for *magnitude, body, motion, time, degrees of quality, action, conception, proportion, speech and names* (in which all the kinds of philosophy consist) are capable of addition and substraction. Now such things as we add or substract, that is, which we put into an account, we are said to *consider*, in Greek λογίζεσθαι, in which language also συλλογίζεσθαι signifies to *compute, reason,* or *reckon.*

4. But *effects* and the *appearances* of things to sense, are faculties or powers of bodies, which make us distinguish them from one another; that is to say, conceive one body to be equal or unequal, like or unlike to another body; as in the example above, when by coming near enough to any body, we perceive the motion and going of the same, we distinguish it thereby from a tree, a column, and other fixed bodies; and so that motion or going is the *property* thereof, as being proper to living creatures, and a faculty by which they make us distinguish them from other bodies.

5. How the knowledge of any effect may be gotten from the knowledge of the generation thereof, may easily be understood by the example of a circle: for if there be set before us a plain figure, having, as near as may be, the figure of a circle, we cannot possibly perceive by sense whether it be a true circle or no; than which, nevertheless, nothing is more easy to be known to him that knows first the generation of the propounded figure. For let it be known that the figure

was made by the circumduction of a body whereof one end remained unmoved, and we may reason thus; a body carried about, retaining always the same length, applies itself first to one *radius,* then to another, to a third, a fourth, and successively to all; and, therefore, the same length, from the same point, toucheth the circumference in every part thereof, which is as much as to say, as all the *radii* are equal. We know, therefore, that from such generation proceeds a figure, from whose one middle point all the extreme points are reached unto by equal *radii.* And in like manner, by knowing first what figure is set before us, we may come by ratiocination to some generation of the same, though perhaps not that by which it was made, yet that by which it might have been made; for he that knows that a circle has the property above declared, will easily know whether a body carried about, as is said, will generate a circle or no.

6. The *end* or *scope* of philosophy is, that we may make use to our benefit of effects formerly seen; or that, by application of bodies to one another, we may produce the like effects of those we conceive in our mind, as far forth as matter, strength, and industry, will permit, for the commodity of human life. For the inward glory and triumph of mind that a man may have for the mastering of some difficult and doubtful matter, or for the discovery of some hidden truth, is not worth so much pains as the study of Philosophy requires; nor need any man care much to teach another what he knows himself, if he think that will be the only benefit of his labour. The end of knowledge is power; and the use of theorems (which, among geometricians, serve for the finding out of properties) is for the construction of problems; and, lastly, the

scope of all speculation is the performing of some action, or thing to be done.

7. But what the *utility* of philosophy is, especially of natural philosophy and geometry, will be best understood by reckoning up the chief commodities of which mankind is capable, and by comparing the manner of life of such as enjoy them, with that of others which want the same. Now, the greatest commodities of mankind are the arts; namely, of measuring matter and motion; of moving ponderous bodies; of architecture; of navigation; of making instruments for all uses; of calculating the celestial motions, the aspects of the stars, and the parts of time; of geography, &c. By which sciences, how great benefits men receive is more easily understood than expressed. These benefits are enjoyed by almost all the people of Europe, by most of those of Asia, and by some of Africa: but the Americans, and they that live near the Poles, do totally want them. But why? Have they sharper wits than these? Have not all men one kind of soul, and the same faculties of mind? What, then, makes this difference, except philosophy? Philosophy, therefore, is the cause of all these benefits. But the utility of moral and civil philosophy is to be estimated, not so much by the commodities we have by knowing these sciences, as by the calamities we receive from not knowing them. Now, all such calamities as may be avoided by human industry, arise from war, but chiefly from civil war; for from this proceed slaughter, solitude, and the want of all things. But the cause of war is not that men are willing to have it; for the will has nothing for object but good, at least that which seemeth good. Nor is it from this, that men know not that the effects of war are evil; for who is there that thinks not poverty

and loss of life to be great evils? The cause, therefore, of civil war is, that men know not the causes neither of war nor peace, there being but few in the world that have learned those duties which unite and keep men in peace, that is to say, that have learned the rules of civil life sufficiently. Now, the knowledge of these rules is moral philosophy. But why have they not learned them, unless for this reason, that none hitherto have taught them in a clear and exact method? For what shall we say? Could the ancient masters of Greece, Egypt, Rome, and others, persuade the unskilful multitude to their innumerable opinions concerning the nature of their gods, which they themselves know not whether they were true or false, and which were indeed manifestly false and absurd; and could they not persuade the same multitude to civil duty, if they themselves had understood it? Or shall those few writings of geometricians which are extant, be thought sufficient for the taking away of all controversy in the matters they treat of, and shall those innumerable and huge volumes of *ethics* be thought unsufficient, if what they teach had been certain and well demonstrated? What, then, can be imagined to be the cause that the writings of those men have increased science, and the writings of these have increased nothing but words, saving that the former were written by men that knew, and the latter by such as know not, the doctrine they taught only for ostentation of their wit and eloquence? Nevertheless, I deny not but the reading of some such books is very delightful; for they are most eloquently written, and contain many clear, wholesome and choice sentences, which yet are not universally true, though by them universally pronounced. From whence it comes to pass, that the circumstances of times, places, and persons being being changed, they are no less frequently made use of to confirm wicked men in their purposes, than to make them understand the precepts of civil duties. Now that which is chiefly wanting in them, is a true and certain rule of our actions, by which we might know whether that we undertake be just or unjust. For it is to no purpose to be bidden in every thing to do right, before there be a certain rule and measure of right established, which no man hitherto hath established. Seeing, therefore, from the not knowing of civil duties, that is, from the want of moral science, proceed civil wars, and the greatest calamities of mankind, we may very well attribute to such science the production of the contrary commodities. And thus much is sufficient, to say nothing of the praises and other contentment proceeding from philosophy, to let you see the utility of the same in every kind thereof.

8. The *subject* of Philosophy, or the matter it treats of, is every body of which we can conceive any generation, and which we may, by any consideration thereof, compare with other bodies, or which is capable of composition and resolution; that is to say, every body of whose generation or properties we can have any knowledge. And this may be deduced from the definition of philosophy, whose profession it is to search out the properties of bodies from their generation, or their generation from their properties; and, therefore, where there is no generation or property, there is no philosophy. Therefore it excludes *Theology,* I mean the doctrine of God, eternal, ingenerable, incomprehensible, and in whom there is nothing neither to divide nor compound, nor any generation to be conceived.

It excludes the doctrine of *angels,* and all such things

as are thought to be neither bodies nor properties of bodies; there being in them no place neither for composition nor division, nor any capacity of more and less, that is to say, no place for ratiocination.

It excludes *history,* as well *natural* as *political,* though most useful (nay necessary) to philosophy; because such knowledge is but experience, or authority, and not ratiocination.

It excludes all such knowledge as is acquired by Divine inspiration, or revelation, as not derived to us by reason, but by Divine grace in an instant, and, as it were, by some sense supernatural.

It excludes not only all doctrines which are false, but such also as are not well-grounded; for whatsoever we know by right ratiocination, can neither be false nor doubtful; and, therefore, *astrology,* as it is now held forth, and all such divinations rather than sciences, are excluded.

Lastly, the doctrine of *God's worship* is excluded from philosophy, as being not to be known by natural reason, but by the authority of the Church; and as being the object of faith, and not of knowledge.

9. The principal parts of philosophy are two. For two chief kinds of bodies, and very different from one another, offer themselves to such as search after their generation and properties; one whereof being the work of nature, is called a *natural body,* the other is called a *commonwealth,* and is made by the wills and agreement of men. And from these spring the two parts of philosophy, called *natural* and *civil.* But seeing that, for the knowledge of the properties of a commonwealth, it is necessary first to know the dispositions, affections, and manners of men, civil philosophy is again commonly divided into two parts, whereof one,

which treats of men's dispositions and manners, is called *ethics;* and the other, which takes cognizance of their civil duties, is called *politics,* or simply *civil philosophy.* In the first place, therefore (after I have set down such premises as appertain to the nature of philosophy in general), I will discourse of *bodies natural;* in the second, of the *dispositions and manners of men;* and in the third, of the *civil duties of subjects.**

10. To conclude; seeing there may be many who will not like this my definition of philosophy, and will say, that, from the liberty which a man may take of so defining as seems best to himself, he may conclude any thing from any thing (though I think it no hard matter to demonstrate that this definition of mine agrees with the sense of all men); yet, lest in this point there should be any cause of dispute betwixt me and them, I here undertake no more than to deliver the elements of that science by which the effects of anything may be found out from the known generation of the same, or contrarily, the generation from the effects; to the end that they who search after other philosophy, may be admonished to seek it from other principles.

CHAPTER II.

OF NAMES.

1. The necessity of sensible Moniments or Marks for the help of Memory: a Mark defined.—2. The necessity of Marks for the signification of the conceptions of the Mind.—3. Names supply both these necessities.—4. The Definition of a Name. —5. Names are Signs not of Things, but of our Cogitations. —6. What it is we give Names to.—7. Names Positive and

---

* For lists of the writings of Hobbes on ethics and on politics, cf. p. xviii.

Negative.—8. Contradictory Names.—9. A Common Name. —10. Names of the First and Second Intention.—11. Universal, Particular, Individual, and Indefinite Names.—12. Names Univocal and Equivocal.—13. Absolute and Relative Names.—14. Simple and Compounded Names.—15. A Predicament described.—16. Some things to be noted concerning Predicaments.

CHAPTER III.

OF PROPOSITION.

1. Divers kinds of speech.—2. Proposition defined.—3. Subject, predicate, and copula, what they are; and abstract and concrete what. The use and abuse of names abstract.—5. Proposition, universal and particular.—6. Affirmative and negative.—7. True and false.—8. True and false belongs to speech, and not to things.—9. Proposition, primary, not primary, definition, axiom, petition.—10. Proposition, necessary and contingent.—11. Categorical and hypothetical.—12. The same proposition diversely pronounced.—13. Propositions that may be reduced to the same categorical proposition, are equipollent.—14. Universal propositions converted by contradictory names, are equipollent.—15. Negative propositions are the same, whether negation be before or after the copula. —16. Particular propositions simply converted, are equipollent.—17. What are subaltern, contrary, subcontrary, and contradictory propositions.—18. Consequence, what it is.—19. Falsity cannot follow from truth.—20. How one proposition is the cause of another.

CHAPTER IV.

OF SYLLOGISM.

1. The definition of syllogism.—2. In a syllogism there are but three terms.—3. Major, minor, and middle term; also major and minor proposition, what they are.—4. The middle term in every syllogism ought to be determined in both the prop-

ositions to one and the same thing.—5. From two particular propositions nothing can be concluded.—6. A syllogism is the collection of two propositions into one sum.—7. The figure of a syllogism, what it is.—8. What is in the mind answering to a syllogism.—9. The first indirect figure, how it is made.—10. The second indirect figure, how made.—11. How the third indirect figure is made.—12. There are many moods in every figure, but most of them useless in philosophy.—13. An hypothetical syllogism when equipollent to a categorical.

CHAPTER V.

OF ERRING, FALSITY, AND CAPTIONS.

1. Erring and falsity, how they differ. Error of the mind by itself without the use of words, how it happens.—2. A sevenfold incoherency of names, every one of which makes always a false proposition.—3. Examples of the first manner of incoherency.—4. Of the second.—5. Of the third.—6. Of the fourth.—7. Of the fifth.—8. Of the sixth.—9. Of the seventh. 10. Falsity of propositions detected by resolving the terms with definitions continued till they come to simple names, or names that are the most general of their kind.—11. Of the fault of a syllogism consisting of the implication of the terms with the copula.—12. Of the fault which consists in equivocation.—13. Sophistical captions are oftener faulty in the matter than in the form of syllogisms.

CHAPTER VI.

OF METHOD.

1. Method and science defined.—2. It is more easily known concerning singular, than universal things, that they are; and contrarily, it is more easily known concerning universal, than singular things, why they are, or what are their causes.—3. What it is philosophers seek to know.—4. The first part, by which principles are found out, is purely analytical.—5. The highest causes, and most universal in every kind, are

known by themselves.—6. Method from principles found out, tending to science simply, what it is.—7. That method of civil and natural science, which proceeds from sense to principles, is analytical; and again, that, which begins at principles, is synthetical.—8. The method of searching out, whether any thing propounded be matter or accident.—9. The method of seeking whether any accident be in this, or in that subject.—10. The method of searching after the cause of any effect propounded.—11. Words serve to invention, as marks; to demonstration, as signs.—12. The method of demonstration is synthetical.—13. Definitions only are primary and universal propositions.—14. The nature and definition of a definition.—15. The properties of a definition.—16. The nature of a demonstration.—17. The properties of a demonstration, and order of things to be demonstrated.—18. The faults of a demonstration.—19. Why the analytical method of geometricians cannot be treated of in this place.

1. For the understanding of *method,* it will be necessary for me to repeat the definition of philosophy, delivered above (Chap. 1, art. 2.) in this manner, *Philosophy is the knowledge we acquire, by true ratiocination, of appearances, or apparent effects, from the knowledge we have of some possible production or generation of the same; and of such production, as has been or may be, from the knowledge we have of the effects.* Method, therefore, in the study of philosophy, *is the shortest way of finding out effects by their known causes, or of causes by their known effects.* But we are then said to know any effect, when we know *that there be causes of the same,* and *in what subject those causes are,* and *in what subject they produce that effect,* and *in what manner they work the same.* And this is the science of causes, or, as they call it, of the διότι. All other science, which is called the ὅτι, is either perception by sense, or the imagination, or memory remaining after such perception.

The first beginnings, therefore, of knowledge, are the phantasms of sense and imagination; and that there be such phantasms we know well enough by nature; but to know why they be, or from what causes they proceed, is the work of ratiocination; which consists (as is said above, in the 1st Chapter, Art. 2) in *composition*, and *division* or *resolution*. There is therefore no method, by which we find out the causes of things, but is either *compositive* or *resolutive*, or *partly compositive*, and *partly resolutive*. And the resolutive is commonly called *analytical* method, as the compositive is called *synthetical*.

2.* It is common to all sorts of method, to proceed from known things to unknown; and this is manifest from the cited definition of philosophy. But in knowledge by sense, the whole object is more known, than any part thereof; as when we see a man, the conception or whole idea of that man is first or more known, than the particular ideas of his being *figurate, animate,* and *rational;* that is, we first see the whole man, and take notice of his being, before we observe in him those other particulars. And therefore in any knowledge of the ὅτι, or that any thing *is*, the beginning of our search is from the whole idea; and contrarily, in our knowledge of the διότι, or of the causes of any thing, that is, in the sciences, we have more knowledge of the causes of the parts than of the whole. For the cause of the whole is compounded of the causes of the parts; but it is necessary that we know the things that are to be compounded, before we can know the whole compound. Now, by parts, I do not here mean parts of the thing itself, but parts of its nature; as, by the parts of man, I do not understand his head, his shoulders, his arms, &c. but his figure, quantity, motion, sense, reason, and the like; which accidents being compounded or put together, constitute the whole nature of man, but not the man himself. And this is the meaning of that common saying, namely, that some things are more known to us, others more known to nature; for I do not think that they, which so distinguish, mean that something is known to nature, which is known to no man; and therefore, by those things, that are more known to us, we are to understand things we take notice of by our senses, and, by more known to nature, those we acquire the knowledge of by reason; for in this sense it is, that the *whole,* that is, those things that have universal names, (which, for brevity's sake, I call *universal*) are more known to us than the *parts,* that is, such things as have names less universal, (which I therefore call *singular*); and the causes of the parts are more known to nature than the cause of the whole; that is, universals than singulars.

3. In the study of philosophy, men search after science either simply or indefinitely; that is, to know as much as they can, without propounding to themselves any limited question; or they enquire into the cause of some determined appearance, or endeavour to find out the certainty of something in question, as what is the cause of *light,* of *heat,* of *gravity,* of a *figure* propounded, and the like; or in what *subject* any propounded *accident* is inherent; or what may conduce most to the *generation* of some propounded *effect* from many *accidents;* or in what manner particular causes ought to be compounded for the production of some certain effect. Now, according to this variety of things in question, sometimes the *analytical method* is to be used, and sometimes the *synthetical.*

4. But to those that search after science indefinitely, which consists in the knowledge of the causes of all things, as far forth as it may be attained, (and the causes of singular things are compounded of the causes of universal or simple things) it is necessary that they know the causes of universal things, or of such accidents as are common to all bodies, that is, to all matter, before they can know the causes of singular things, that is, of those accidents by which one thing is distinguished from another. And, again, they must know what those universal things are, before they can know their causes. Moreover, seeing universal things are contained in the nature of singular things, the knowledge of them is to be acquired by reason, that is, by resolution. For example, if there be propounded a conception or *idea* of some singular thing, as of a *square*, this square is to be resolved into a *plain, terminated with a certain number of equal and straight lines and right angles.* For by this resolution we have these things universal or agreeable to all matter, namely, *line, plain,* (which contains *superficies*) *terminated, angle, straightness, rectitude,* and *equality;* and if we can find out the causes of these, we may compound them altogether into the cause of a square. Again, if any man propound to himself the conception of *gold,* he may, by resolving, come to the ideas of *solid, visible, heavy,* (that is, tending to the centre of the earth, or downwards) and many other more universal than gold itself; and these he may resolve again, till he come to such things as are most universal. And in this manner, by resolving continually, we may come to know what those things are, whose causes being first known severally, and afterwards compounded, bring us to the knowledge of singular things. I conclude,

therefore, that the method of attaining to the universal knowledge of things, is purely *analytical.*

5. But the causes of universal things (of those, at least, that have any cause) are manifest of themselves, or (as they say commonly) known to nature; so that they need no method at all; for they have all but one universal cause, which is motion. For the variety of all figures arises out of the variety of those motions by which they are made; and motion cannot be understood to have any other cause besides motion; nor has the variety of those things we perceive by sense, as of *colours, sounds, savours,* &c. any other cause than motion, residing partly in the objects that work upon our senses, and partly in ourselves, in such manner, as that it is manifestly some kind of motion, though we cannot, without ratiocination, come to know what kind. For though many cannot understand till it be in some sort demonstrated to them, that all mutation consists in motion; yet this happens not from any obscurity in the thing itself, (for it is not intelligible that anything can depart either from rest, or from the motion it has, except by motion), but either by having their natural discourse corrupted with former opinions received from their masters, or else for this, that they do not at all bend their mind to the enquiring out of truth.

6. By the knowledge therefore of universals, and of their causes (which are the first principles by which we know the διότι of things) we have in the first place their definitions, (which are nothing but the explication of our simple conceptions.) For example, he that has a true conception of *place,* cannot be ignorant of this definition, *place is that space which is possessed or filled adequately by some body;* and so, he that conceives *motion* aright, cannot but know that *motion is*

the privation of one place, and the acquisition of another. In the next place, we have their generations or descriptions; as (for example) that *a line is made by the motion of a point, superficies by the motion of a line,* and *one motion by another motion,* &c. It remains, that we enquire what motion begets such and such effects; as, what motion makes a straight line, and what a circular; what motion thrusts, what draws, and by what way; what makes a thing which is seen or heard, to be seen or heard sometimes in one manner, sometimes in another. Now the method of this kind of enquiry, is *compositive.* For first, we are to observe what effect a body moved produceth, when we consider nothing in it besides its motion; and we see presently that this makes a line, or length; next, what the motion of a long body produces, which we find to be superficies; and so forwards, till we see what the effects of simple motion are; and then, in like manner, we are to observe what proceeds from the addition, multiplication, substraction, and division, of these motions, and what effects, what figures, and what propertics, they produce; from which kind of contemplation sprung that part of philosophy which is called *geometry.*

From this consideration of what is produced by simple motion, we are to pass to the consideration of what effects one body moved worketh upon another; and because there may be motion in all the several parts of a body, yet so as that the whole body remain still in the same place, we must enquire first, what motion causeth such and such motion in the whole, that is, when one body invades another body which is either at rest or in motion, what way, and with what swiftness, the invaded body shall move; and, again, what motion this second body will generate in a third, and so forwards. From which contemplation shall be drawn that part of philosophy which treats of motion.

In the third place we must proceed to the enquiry of such effects as are made by the motion of the parts of any body, as, how it comes to pass, that things when they are the same, yet seem not to be the same, but changed. And here the things we search after are sensible qualities, such as *light, colour, transparency, opacity, sound, odour, savour, heat, cold,* and the like; which because they cannot be known till we know the causes of sense itself, therefore the consideration of the causes of *seeing, hearing, smelling, tasting* and *touching,* belongs to this third place; and all those qualities and changes, above mentioned, are to be referred to the fourth place; which two considerations comprehend that part of philosophy which is called *physics.* And in these four parts is contained whatsoever in natural philosophy may be explicated by demonstration, properly so called. For if a cause were to be rendered of natural appearances in special, as, what are the motions and influences of the heavenly bodies, and of their parts, the reason hereof must either be drawn from the parts of the sciences above mentioned, or no reason at all will be given, but all left to uncertain conjecture.

After *physics* we must come to *moral philosophy;* in which we are to consider the motions of the mind, namely, *appetite, aversion, love, benevolence, hope, fear, anger, emulation, envy,* &c.; what causes they have, and of what they be causes. And the reason why these are to be considered after *physics* is, that they have their causes in sense and imagination, which are the subject of *physical* contemplation. Also the reason, why all these things are to be searched after in the order above-said, is, that physics cannot be understood, except we know first what motions are in the smallest parts of bodies; nor such motion of parts, till we know what it is that makes another body move; nor this, till we know what simple motion will effect. And because all appearance of things to sense is determined, and made to be of such and such quality and quantity by compounded motions, every one of which has a certain degree of velocity, and a certain and determined way; therefore, in the first place, we are to search out the ways of motion simply (in which geometry consists); next the ways of such generated motions as are manifest; and, lastly, the ways of internal and invisible motions (which is the enquiry of natural philosophers). And, therefore, they that study natural philosophy, study in vain, except they begin at geometry; and such writers or disputers thereof, as are ignorant of geometry, do but make their readers and hearers lose their time.

7. *Civil* and *moral philosophy* do not so adhere to one another, but that they may be severed. For the causes of the motions of the mind are known, not only by ratiocination, but also by the experience of every man that takes the pains to observe those motions within himself. And, therefore, not only they that have attained the knowledge of the passions and perturbations of the mind, by the *synthetical method,* and from the very first principles of philosophy, may by proceeding in the same way, come to the causes and necessity of constituting commonwealths, and to get the knowledge of what is natural right, and what are civil duties; and, in every kind of government, what are the rights of the commonwealth, and all other

knowledge appertaining to civil philosophy; for this reason, that the principles of the politics consist in the knowledge of the motions of the mind, and the knowledge of these motions from the knowledge of sense and imagination; but even they also that have not learned the first part of philosophy, namely, *geometry* and *physics,* may, notwithstanding, attain the principles of civil philosophy, by the *analytical method.* For if a question be propounded, as, *whether such an action be just or unjust;* if that *unjust* be resolved into *fact against law,* and that notion *law* into the *command* of him or them that have *coercive power;* and that *power* be derived from the *wills* of men that constitute such power, to the end they may live in peace, they may at last come to this, that the appetites of men and the passions of their minds are such, that, unless they be restrained by some power, they will always be making war upon one another; which may be known to be so by any man's experience, that will but examine his own mind. And, therefore, from hence he may proceed, by compounding, to the determination of the justice or injustice of any propounded action. So that it is manifest, by what has been said, that the method of philosophy, to such as seek science simply, without propounding to themselves the solution of any particular question, is partly analytical, and partly synthetical; namely, that which proceeds from sense to the invention of principles, analytical; and the rest synthetical.

8. To those that seek the cause of some certain and propounded appearance or effect, it happens, sometimes, that they know not whether the thing, whose cause is sought after, be matter or body, or some accident of a body. For though in geometry, when the cause is sought of magnitude, or proportion, or figure,

it be certainly known that these things, namely magnitude, proportion, and figure, are accidents; yet in natural philosophy, where all questions are concerning the causes of the phantasms of sensible things, it is not so easy to discern between the things themselves, from which those phantasms proceed, and the appearances of those things to the sense; which have deceived many, especially when the phantasms have been made by light. For example, a man that looks upon the sun, has a certain shining idea of the magnitude of about a foot over, and this he calls the sun, though he know the sun to be truly a great deal bigger; and, in like manner, the phantasm of the same thing appears sometimes round, by being seen afar off, and sometimes square, by being nearer. Whereupon it may well be doubted, whether that phantasm be matter, or some body natural, or only some accident of a body; in the examination of which doubt we may use this method. The properties of matter and accidents already found out by us, by the synthetical method, from their definitions, are to be compared with the idea we have before us; and if it agree with the properties of matter or body, then it is a body; otherwise it is an accident. Seeing, therefore, matter cannot by any endeavor of ours be either made or destroyed, or increased, or diminished, or moved out of its place, whereas that idea appears, vanishes, is increased and diminished, and moved hither and thither at pleasure; we may certainly conclude that it is not a body, but an accident only. And this method is *synthetical.*

9. But if there be a doubt made concerning the subject of any known accident (for this may be doubted sometimes, as in the precedent example, doubt may be made in what subject that splendour and apparent

magnitude of the sun is), then our enquiry must proceed in this manner. First, matter in general must be divided into parts, as, into object, medium, and the sentient itself, or such other parts as seem most conformable to the thing propounded. Next, these parts are severally to be examined how they agree with the definition of the subject; and such of them as are not capable of that accident are to be rejected. For example, if by any true ratiocination the sun be found to be greater than its apparent magnitude, then that magnitude is not in the sun; if the sun be in one determined straight line, and one determined distance, and the magnitude and splendour be seen in more lines and distances than one, as it is in reflection or refraction, then neither that splendour nor apparent magnitude are in the sun itself, and, therefore, the body of the sun cannot be the subject of that splendour and magnitude. And for the same reasons the air and other parts will be rejected, till at last nothing remain which can be the subject of that splendour and magnitude but the sentient itself. And this method, in regard the subject is divided into parts, is analytical; and in regard the properties, both of the subject and accident, are compared with the accident concerning whose subject the enquiry is made, it is synthetical.

10. But when we seek after the cause of any propounded effect, we must in the first place get into our mind an exact notion or idea of that which we call cause, namely, that *a cause is the sum or aggregate of all such accidents, both in the agents and the patient, as concur to the producing of the effect propounded; all of which existing together, it cannot be understood but that the effect existeth with them; or that it can possibly exist if any one of them be absent.* This being

known, in the next place we must examine singly every accident that accompanies or precedes the effect, as far forth as it seems to conduce in any manner to the production of the same, and see whether the propounded effect may be conceived to exist, without the existence of any of those accidents; and by this means separate such accidents, as do not concur, from such as concur to produce the said effect; which being done, we are to put together the concurring accidents, and consider whether we can possibly conceive, that when these are all present, the effect propounded will not follow; and if it be evident that the effect will follow, then that aggregate of accidents is the entire cause, otherwise not; but we must still search out and put together other accidents. For example, if the cause of light be propounded to be sought out; first, we examine things without us, and find that whensoever light appears, there is some principal object, as it were the fountain of light, without which we cannot have any perception of light; and, therefore, the concurrence of that object is necessary to the generation of light. Next we consider the medium, and find, that unless it be disposed in a certain manner, namely, that it be transparent, though the object remain the same, yet the effect will not follow; and, therefore, the concurrence of transparency is also necessary to the generation of light. Thirdly, we observe our own body, and find that by the indisposition of the eyes, the brain, the nerves, and the heart, that is, by obstructions, stupidity, and debility we are deprived of light, so that a fitting disposition of the organs to receive impressions from without is likewise a necessary part of the cause of light. Again, of all the accidents inherent in the object, there is none that can conduce to the effecting of light, but only action (or a certain motion), which cannot be conceived to be wanting, whensoever the effect is present; for, that anything may shine, it is not requisite that it be of such or such magnitude or figure, or that the whole body of it be moved out of the place it is in (unless it may perhaps be said, that in the sun, or other body, that which causes light is the light it hath in itself; which yet is but a trifling exception, seeing nothing is meant thereby but the cause of light; as if any man should say that the cause of light is that in the sun which produceth it); it remains, therefore, that the action, by which light is generated, is motion only in the parts of the object. Which being understood, we may easily conceive what it is the medium contributes, namely, the continuation of that motion to the eye; and, lastly, what the eye and the rest of the organs of the sentient contribute, namely, the continuation of the same motion to the last organ of sense, the heart. And in this manner the cause of light may be made up of motion continued from the original of the same motion, to the original of vital motion, light being nothing but the alteration of vital motion, made by the impression upon it of motion continued from the object. But I give this only for an example, for I shall speak more at large of light, and the generation of it, in its proper place. In the mean time it is manifest, that in the searching out of causes, there is need partly of the analytical, and partly of the synthetical method; of the analytical, to conceive how circumstances conduce severally to the production of effects; and of the synthetical, for the adding together and compounding of what they can effect singly by themselves. And thus much may serve for the method of invention. It remains that I speak of the method of teaching, that is, of demonstration, and of the means by which we demonstrate.

11. In the method of invention, the use of words consists in this, that they may serve for marks, by which, whatsoever we have found out may be recalled to memory; for without this all our inventions perish, nor will it be possible for us to go on from principles beyond a syllogism or two, by reason of the weakness of memory. For example, if any man, by considering a triangle set before him, should find that all its angles together taken are equal to two right angles, and that by thinking of the same tacitly, without any use of words either understood or expressed; and it should happen afterwards that another triangle, unlike the former, or the same in different situation, should be offered to his consideration, he would not know readily whether the same property were in this last or no, but would be forced, as often as a different triangle were brought before him (and the difference of triangles is infinite) to begin his contemplation anew; which he would have no need to do if he had the use of names, for every universal name denotes the conceptions we have of infinite singular things. Nevertheless, as I said above, they serve as *marks* for the help of our memory, whereby we register to ourselves our own inventions; but not as *signs* by which we declare the same to others; so that a man may be a philosopher alone by himself, without any master; Adam had this capacity. But to teach, that is, to demonstrate, supposes two at the least, and syllogistical speech.

12. And seeing teaching is nothing but leading the mind of him we teach, to the knowledge of our inventions, in that track by which we attained the same with our own mind; therefore, the same method that

served for our invention, will serve also for demonstration to others, saving that we omit the first part of method which proceeded from the sense of things to universal principles, which, because they are principles, cannot be demonstrated; and seeing they are known by nature, (as was said above in the 5th article) they need no demonstration, though they need explication. The whole method, therefore, of demonstration, is *synthetical,* consisting of that order of speech which begins from primary or most universal propositions, which are manifest of themselves, and proceeds by a perpetual composition of propositions into syllogisms, till at last the learner understand the truth of the conclusion sought after.

13. Now, such principles are nothing but definitions, whereof there are two sorts; one of names, that signify such things as have some conceivable cause, and another of such names as signify things of which we can conceive no cause at all. Names of the former kind are, *body,* or *matter, quantity,* or *extension, motion,* and whatsoever is common to all matter. Of the second kind, are *such a body, such and so great motion, so great magnitude, such figure,* and whatsoever we can distinguish one body from another by. And names of the former kind are well enough defined, when, by speech as short as may be, we raise in the mind of the hearer perfect and clear ideas or conceptions of the things named, as when we define motion to be *the leaving of one place, and the acquiring of another continually;* for though no thing moved, nor any cause of motion be in that definition, yet, at the hearing of that speech, there will come into the mind of the hearer an *idea* of motion clear enough. But definitions of things, which may be understood to have

some cause, must consist of such names as express the cause or manner of their generation, as when we define a circle to be a figure made by the circumduction of a straight line in a plane, &c. Besides definitions, there is no other proposition that ought to be called primary, or (according to severe truth) be received into the number of principles. For those *axioms of Euclid,* seeing they may be demonstrated, are no principles of demonstration, though they have by the consent of all men gotten the authority of principles, because they need not be demonstrated. Also, those *petitions,* or *postulata,* (as they call them) though they be principles, yet they are not principles of demonstration, but of construction only; that is, not of science, but of power; or (which is all one) not of *theorems,* which are speculations, but of *problems,* which belong to practice, or the doing of something. But as for those common received opinions, *Nature abhors vacuity, Nature doth nothing in vain,* and the like, which are neither evident in themselves, nor at all to be demonstrated, and which are oftener false than true, they are much less to be acknowledged for principles.

To return, therefore, to definitions; the reason why I say that the cause and generation of such things, as have any cause or generation, ought to enter into their definitions, is this. The end of science is the demonstration of the causes and generation of things; which if they be not in the definitions, they cannot be found in the conclusion of the first syllogism, that is made from those definitions; and if they be not in the first conclusion, they will not be found in any further conclusion deduced from that; and, therefore, by proceeding in this manner, we shall never come to science;

which is against the scope and intention of demonstration.

14. Now, seeing definitions (as I have said) are principles, or primary propositions, they are therefore speeches; and seeing they are used for the raising of an *idea* of some thing in the mind of the learner, whensoever that thing has a name, the definition of it can be nothing but the explication of that name by speech; and if that name be given it for some compounded conception, the definition is nothing but a resolution of that name into its most universal parts. As when we define man, saying *man is a body animated, sentient, rational,* those names, *body animated,* &c., are parts of that whole name *man;* so that definitions of this kind always consist of *genus* and *difference;* the former names being all, till the last, *general;* and the last of all, *difference.* But if any name be the most universal in its kind, then the definition of it cannot consist of *genus* and *difference,* but is to be made by such circumlocution, as best explicateth the force of that name. Again, it is possible, and happens often, that the *genus* and *difference* are put together, and yet make no definition; as these words, *a straight line,* contain both the *genus* and *difference;* but are not a definition, unless we should think a straight line may be thus defined, *a straight line is a straight line:* and yet if there were added another name, consisting of different words, but signifying the same thing which these signify, then these might be the definition of that name. From what has been said, it may be understood how a definition ought to be defined, namely, *that it is a proposition, whose predicate resolves the subject, when it may; and when it may not, it exemplifies the same.*

15. The properties of a definition are:

First, that it takes away equivocation, as also all that multitude of distinctions, which are used by such as think they may learn philosophy by disputation. For the nature of a definition is to define, that is, to determine the signification of the defined name, and to pare from it all other signification besides what is contained in the definition itself; and therefore one definition does as much, as all the distinctions (how many soever) that can be used about the name defined.

Secondly, that it gives an universal notion of the thing defined, representing a certain universal picture thereof, not to the eye, but to the mind. For as when one paints a man, he paints the image of some man; so he, that defines the name man, makes a representation of some man to the mind.

Thirdly, that it is not necessary to dispute whether definitions are to be admitted or no. For when a master is instructing his scholar, if the scholar understand all the parts of the thing defined, which are resolved in the definition, and yet will not admit of the definition, there needs no further controversy betwixt them, it being all one as if he refused to be taught. But if he understand nothing, then certainly the definition is faulty; for the nature of a definition consists in this, that it exhibit a clear idea of the thing defined; and principles are either known by themselves, or else they are not principles.

Fourthly, that, in philosophy, definitions are before defined names. For in teaching philosophy, the first beginning is from definitions; and all progression in the same, till we come to the knowledge of the thing compounded, is compositive. Seeing, therefore, definition is the explication of a compounded name by resolution, and the progression is from the parts to the compound, definitions must be understood before compounded names; nay, when the names of the parts of any speech be explicated, it is not necessary that the definition should be a name compounded of them. For example, when these names, *equilateral, quadrilateral, right-angled*, are sufficiently understood, it is not necessary in geometry that there should be at all such a name as *square;* for defined names are received in philosophy for brevity's sake only.

Fifthly, that compounded names, which are defined one way in some one part of philosophy, may in another part of the same be otherwise defined; as a *parabola* and an *hyperbole* have one definition in geometry, and another in rhetoric; for definitions are instituted and serve for the understanding of the doctrine which is treated of. And, therefore, as in one part of philosophy, a definition may have in it some one fit name for the more brief explanation of some proposition in geometry; so it may have the same liberty in other parts of philosophy; for the use of names is particular (even where many agree to the settling of them) and arbitrary.

Sixthly, that no name can be defined by any one word; because no one word is sufficient for the resolving of one or more words.

Seventhly, that a defined name ought not to be repeated in the definition. For a defined name is the whole compound, and a definition is the resolution of that compound into parts; but no total can be part of itself.

16. Any two definitions, that may be compounded into a syllogism, produce a conclusion; which, because it is derived from principles, that is, from definitions, is said to be demonstrated; and the derivation or com-

position itself is called a demonstration. In like manner, if a syllogism be made of two propositions, whereof one is a definition, the other a demonstrated conclusion, or neither of them is a definition, but both formerly demonstrated, that syllogism is also called a demonstration, and so successively. The definition therefore of a demonstration is this, *a demonstration is a syllogism, or series of syllogisms, derived and continued, from the definitions of names, to the last conclusion.* And from hence it may be understood, that all true ratiocination, which taketh its beginning from true principles, produceth science, and is true demonstration. For as for the original of the name, although that, which the Greeks called ἀπόδειξις, and the Latins *demonstratio,* was understood by them for that sort only of ratiocination, in which, by the describing of certain lines and figures, they placed the thing they were to prove, as it were before men's eyes, which is properly ἀποδεικνύειν, or to *shew* by the figure; yet they seem to have done it for this reason, that unless it were in geometry, (in which only there is place for such figures) there was no ratiocination certain, and ending in science, their doctrines concerning all other things being nothing but controversy and clamour; which, nevertheless, happened, not because the truth to which they pretended could not be made evident without figures, but because they wanted true principles, from which they might derive their ratiocination; and, therefore, there is no reason but that if true definitions were premised in all sorts of doctrines, the demonstrations also would be trne.

17. It is proper to methodical demonstration,

First, that there be a true succession of one reason to

another, according to the rules of syllogizing delivered above.

Secondly, that the premises of all syllogisms be demonstrated from the first definitions.

Thirdly, that after definitions, he that teaches or demonstrates any thing, proceed in the same method by which he found it out; namely, that in the first place those things be demonstrated, which immediately succeed to universal definitions (in which is contained that part of philosophy which is called *philosophia prima*). Next, those things which may be demonstrated by simple motion (in which geometry consists). After geometry, such things as may be taught or shewed by manifest action, that is, by thrusting from, or pulling towards. And after these, the motion or mutation of the invisible parts of things, and the doctrine of sense and imaginations, and of the internal passions, especially those of men, in which are comprehended the grounds of civil duties, or civil philosophy; which takes up the last place. And that this method ought to be kept in all sorts of philosophy, is evident from hence, that such things as I have said are to be taught last, cannot be demonstrated, till such as are propounded to be first treated of, be fully understood. Of which method no other example can be given, but that treatise of the elements of philosophy, which I shall begin in the next chapter, and continue to the end of the work.

18. Besides those *paralogisms*, whose fault lies either in the falsity of the premises, or the want of true composition, of which I have spoken in the precedent chapter, there are two more, which are frequent in demonstration; one whereof is commonly called *petitio principii;* the other is the supposing of a *false cause;*

and these do not only deceive unskilful learners, but sometimes masters themselves, by making them take that for well demonstrated, which is not demonstrated at all. *Petitio principii* is, when the conclusion to be proved is disguised in other words, and put for the definition or principle from whence it is to be demonstrated; and thus, by putting for the cause of the thing sought, either the thing itself or some effect of it, they make a circle in their demonstration. As for example, he that would demonstrate that the earth stands still in the centre of the world, and should suppose the earth's gravity to be the cause thereof, and define gravity to be a quality by which every heavy body tends towards the centre of the world, would lose his labour; for the question is, what is the cause of that quality in the earth? and, therefore, he that supposes gravity to be the cause, puts the thing itself for its own cause.

Of a *false cause* I find this example in a certain treatise where the thing to be demonstrated is the motion of the earth. He begins, therefore, with this, that seeing the earth and the sun are not always in the same situation, it must needs be that one of them be locally moved, which is true; next, he affirms that the vapours which the sun raises from the earth and sea, are, by reason of this motion, necessarily moved, which also is true; from whence he infers the winds are made, and this may pass for granted; and by these winds he says, the waters of the sea are moved, and by their motion the bottom of the sea, as if it were beaten forwards, moves round; and let this also be granted; wherefore, he concludes, the earth is moved; which is, nevertheless, a paralogism. For, if that wind were the cause why the earth was, from the beginning, moved round, and the motion either of the sun or the earth were the cause of that wind, then the motion of the sun or the earth was before the wind itself; and if the earth were moved, before the wind was made, then the wind could not be the cause of the earth's revolution; but, if the sun were moved, and the earth stand still, then it is manifest the earth might remain unmoved, notwithstanding that wind; and therefore that motion was not made by the cause which he allegeth. But paralogisms of this kind are very frequent among the writers of *physics*, though none can be more elaborate than this in the example given.

19. It may to some men seem pertinent to treat in this place of that art of the geometricians, which they call *logistica*, that is, the art, by which, from supposing the thing in question to be true, they proceed by ratiocination, till either they come to something known, by which they may demonstrate the truth of the thing sought for; or to something which is impossible, from whence they collect that to be false, which they supposed true. But this art cannot be explicated here, for this reason, that the method of it can neither be practised, nor understood, unless by such as are well versed in geometry; and among geometricians themselves, they, that have most theorems in readiness, are the most ready in the use of this *logistica;* so that, indeed, it is not a distinct thing for geometry itself; for there are, in the method of it, three parts; the first whereof consists in the finding out of equality betwixt known and unknown things, which they call equation; and this equation cannot be found out, but by such as know perfectly the nature, properties, and transpositions of proportion, as also the addition, subtraction, multiplication, and division of lines and superficies, and the extraction of roots; which are the parts of no mean geo-

metrician. The second is, when an equation is found, to be able to judge whether the truth or falsity of the question may be deduced from it, or no; which yet requires greater knowledge. And the third is, when such an equation is found, as is fit for the solution of the question, to know how to resolve the same in such manner, that the truth or falsity may thereby manifestly appear; which, in hard questions, cannot be done without the knowledge of the nature of crooked-lined figures; but he that understands readily the nature and properties of these, is a complete geometrician. It happens besides, that for the finding out of equations, there is no certain method, but he is best able to do it, that has the best natural wit.

PART II.

THE FIRST GROUNDS OF PHILOSOPHY.

CHAPTER VII.*

OF PLACE AND TIME.

1. Things that have no existence, may nevertheless be understood and computed.—2. What is Space.—3. Time.—4. Part. 5. Division.—6. One.—7. Number.—8. Composition.—9. The whole.—10. Spaces and times contiguous, and continual.—11 Beginning, end, way, finite, infinite.—12. What is infinite in power. Nothing infinite can be truly said to be either whole, or one; nor infinite spaces or times, many.—13. Division proceeds not to the least.

1. In the teaching of natural philosophy, I cannot begin better (as I have already shewn) than from *privation;* that is, from feigning the world to be annihilated. But, if such annihilation of all things be supposed, it may perhaps be asked, what would remain for any man (whom only I except from this universal annihilation of things) to consider as the subject of philosophy, or at all to reason upon; or what to give names unto for ratiocination's sake.

I say, therefore, there would remain to that man

* For parallel passages from the Latin text of chapters VII.-X. of *De Corpore,* cf. pp. 183 *seq.*

ideas of the world, and of all such bodies as he had, before their annihilation, seen with his eyes, or perceived by any other sense; that is to say, the memory and imagination of magnitudes, motions, sounds, colours, &c. as also of their order and parts. All which things, though they be nothing but ideas and phantasms, happening internally to him that imagineth; yet they will appear as if they were external, and not at all depending upon any power of the mind. And these are the things to which he would give names, and subtract them from, and compound them with one another. For seeing, that after the destruction of all other things, I suppose man still remaining, and namely that he thinks, imagines, and remembers, there can be nothing for him to think of but what is past; nay, if we do but observe diligently what it is we do when we consider and reason, we shall find, that though all things be still remaining in the world, yet we compute nothing but our own phantasms. For when we calculate the magnitude and motions of heaven or earth, we do not ascend into heaven that we may divide it into parts, or measure the motions thereof, but we do it sitting still in our closets or in the dark. Now things may be considered, that is, be brought into account, either as internal accidents of our mind, in which manner we consider them when the question is about some faculty of the mind; or as species of external things, not as really existing, but appearing only to exist, or to have a being without us. And in this manner we are now to consider them.

2. If therefore we remember, or have a phantasm of any thing that was in the world before the supposed annihilation of the same; and consider, not that the thing was such or such, but only that it had a being

without the mind, we have presently a conception of that we call *space:* an imaginary space indeed, because a mere phantasm, yet that very thing which all men call so. For no man calls it space for being already filled, but because it may be filled; nor does any man think bodies carry their places away with them, but that the same space contains sometimes one, sometimes another body; which could not be if space should always accompany the body which is once in it. And this is of itself so manifest, that I should not think it needed any explaining at all, but that I find space to be falsely defined by certain philosophers, who infer from thence, one, that the world is infinite (for taking *space* to be the extension of bodies, and thinking extension may encrease continually, he infers that bodies may be infinitely extended); and, another, from the same definition, concludes rashly, that it is impossible even to God himself to create more worlds than one; for, if another world were to be created, he says, that seeing there is nothing without this world, and therefore (according to his definition) no space, that new world must be placed in nothing; but in nothing nothing can be placed; which he affirms only, without showing any reason for the same; whereas the contrary is the truth: for more cannot be put into a place already filled, so much is empty space fitter than that, which is full, for the receiving of new bodies. Having therefore spoken thus much for these men's sakes, and for theirs that assent to them, I return to my purpose, and define *space* thus: SPACE *is the phantasm of a thing existing without the mind simply;* that is to say, that phantasm, in which we consider no other accident, but only that it appears without us.

3. As a body leaves a phantasm of its magnitude in

the mind, so also a moved body leaves a phantasm of its motion, namely, an idea of that body passing out of one space into another by continual succession. And this idea, or phantasm, is that, which (without receding much from the common opinion, or from *Aristotle's* definition) I call *Time*. For seeing all men confess a year to be time, and yet do not think a year to be the accident or affection of any body, they must needs confess it to be, not in the things without us, but only in the thought of the mind. So when they speak of the times of their predecessors, they do not think after their predecessors are gone, that their times can be any where else than in the memory of those that remember them. And as for those that say, days, years, and months are the motions of the sun and moon, seeing it is all one to say, motion *past* and motion *destroyed,* and that *future* motion is the same with motion which *is not yet begun,* they say that, which they do not mean, that there neither is, nor has been, nor shall be any time: for of whatsoever it may be said, *it has been* or *it shall be,* of the same also it might have been said heretofore, or may be said hereafter, *it is.* What then can days, months, and years, be, but the names of such computations made in our mind? *Time* therefore is a phantasm, but a phantasm of motion, for if we would know by what moments time passes away, we make use of some motion or other, as of the sun, of a clock, of the sand in an hourglass, or we mark some line upon which we imagine something to be moved, there being no other means by which we can take notice of any time at all. And yet, when I say *time* is a phantasm of motion, I do not say this is sufficient to define it by; for this word *time* comprehends the notion of *former* and *latter,* or of *succession* in the motion of a body, in as much as it is first *here* then *there*. Wherefore a complete definition of *time* is such as this, TIME *is the phantasm of before and after in motion;* which agrees with this definition of *Aristotle, time is the number of motion according to former and latter;* for that numbering is an act of the mind; and therefore it is all one to say, *time is the number of motion according to former and latter;* and *time is a phantasm of motion numbered.* But that other definition, *time is the measure of motion,* is not so exact, for we measure time by motion and not motion by time.

4. One space is called *part* of another space, and one time *part* of another time, when this contains that and something besides. From whence it may be collected, that nothing can rightly be called a PART, but that which is compared with something that contains it.

5. And therefore to *make parts,* or to *part* or DIVIDE space or *time,* is nothing else but to consider one and another within the same; so that if any man *divide* space or time, the diverse conceptions he has are more, by one, than the parts he makes; for his first conception is of that which is to be divided, then of some part of it, and again of some other part of it, and so forwards as long as he goes on in dividing.

But it is to be noted, that here, by *division,* I do not mean the severing or pulling asunder of one space or time from another (for does any man think that one hemisphere may be separated from the other hemisphere, or the first hour from the second?) but diversity of consideration; so that division is not made by the operation of the hands but of the mind.

6. When space or time is considered among other spaces or times, it is said to be ONE, namely, *one of them;* for except one space might be added to another,

and subtracted from another space, and so of time, it would be sufficient to say space or time simply, and superfluous to say one space or one time, if it could not be conceived that there were another. The common definition of *one,* namely, that *one is that which is undivided,* is obnoxious to an absurd consequence; for it may thence be inferred, that whatsoever is divided is many things, that is, that every divided thing, is divided things, which is insignificant.

7. NUMBER is *one* and *one,* or *one one* and *one,* and so forwards; namely, *one* and *one* make the number *two,* and *one one* and *one* the number *three;* so are all other numbers made; which is all one as if we should say, *number is unities.*

8. To COMPOUND space of spaces, or time of times, is first to consider them one after another, and then altogether as one; as if one should reckon first the head, the feet, the arms, and the body, severally, and then for the account of them all together put *man.* And that which is so put for all the severals of which it consists, is called the WHOLE; and those severals, when by the division of the whole they come again to be considered singly, are parts thereof; and therefore the *whole* and *all the parts taken together* are the same thing. And as I noted above, that in *division* it is not necessary to pull the parts asunder; so in *composition,* it is to be understood, that for the making up of a whole there is no need of putting the parts together, so as to make them touch one another, but only of collecting them into one sum in the mind. For thus all men, being considered together, make up the whole of mankind, though never so much dispersed by time and place; and twelve hours, though the hours of several days, may be compounded into one number of twelve.

9. This being well understood, it is manifest that nothing can rightly be called a whole, that is not conceived to be compounded of parts, and that it may be divided into parts; so that if we deny that a thing has parts, we deny the same to be a whole. For example, if we say the soul can have no parts, we affirm that no soul can be a whole soul. Also it is manifest, that nothing has parts till it be divided; and when a thing is divided, the parts are only so many as the division makes them. Again, that a part of a part is a part of the whole; and thus any part of the number *four,* as *two,* is a part of the number *eight;* for *four* is made of *two* and *two;* but *eight* is compounded of *two, two,* and *four,* and therefore *two,* which is a part of the part *four,* is also a part of the whole *eight.*

10. Two spaces are said to be CONTIGUOUS, when there is no other space betwixt them. But two times, betwixt which there is no other time, are called immediate, as A B, B C. And any two spaces, as well as times, are said to be CONTINUAL, when they have one common part, as A C, B D, where the part B C is common; and more spaces and times are continual, when every two which are next one another are continual.

A B C

A B C D

11. That part which is between two other parts, is called a MEAN; and that which is not between two other parts, an EXTREME. And of extremes, that which is first recokned is the BFGINNING, and that which last, the END; and all the means together taken are the WAY. Also, *extreme parts* and *limits* are the same thing. And from hence it is manifest, that *beginning* and *end* depend upon the order in which we number them; and that to *terminate* or *limit* space and time, is the same

thing with *imagining their beginning and end;* as also that every thing is FINITE or INFINITE, according as we imagine or not imagine it *limited* or *terminated* every way; and that the *limits* of any number are *unities,* and of these, that which is the first in our numbering is the *beginning,* and that which we number last, is the *end.* When we say number is *infinite,* we mean only that no number is expressed; for when we speak of the numbers *two, three, a thousand,* &c. they are always *finite.* But when no more is said but this, *number is infinite,* it is to be understood as if it were said, this name *number* is an *indefinite name.*

12. Space or time is said to be *finite in power,* or *terminable,* when there may be assigned a number of finite spaces or times, as of paces or hours, than which there can be no greater number of the same measure in that space or time; and *infinite in power* is that space or time, in which a greater number of the said paces or hours may be assigned, than any number that can be given. But we must note, that, although in that space or time which is infinite in power, there may be numbered more paces or hours than any number that can be assigned, yet their number will always be finite; for every number is finite. And therefore his ratiocination was not good, that undertaking to prove the world to be finite, reasoned thus: *If the world be infinite, then there may be taken in it some part which is distant from us an infinite number of paces: but no such part can be taken; wherefore the world is not infinite;* because that consequence of the major proposition is false; for in an infinite space, whatsoever we take or design in our mind, the distance of the same from us is a finite space; for in the very designing of the place thereof, we put an end to that space, of which

we ourselves are the beginning; and whatsoever any man with his mind cuts off both ways from infinite, he determines the same, that is, he makes it finite.

Of infinite space or time, it cannot be said that it is a *whole* or *one:* not a *whole,* because not compounded of parts; for seeing parts, how many soever they be, are severally finite, they will also, when they are all put together, make a whole finite: nor *one,* because nothing can be said to be one, except there be another to compare it with; but it cannot be conceived that there are two spaces, or two times, infinite. Lastly, when we make question whether the world be finite or infinite, we have nothing in our mind answering to the name *world;* for whatsoever we imagine, is therefore finite, though our computation reach the fixed stars, or the ninth or tenth, nay, the thousandth sphere. The meaning of the question is this only, whether God has actually made so great an addition of body to body, as we are able to make of space to space.

13. And, therefore, that which is commonly said, that space and time may be divided infinitely, is not to be so understood, as if there might be any infinite or eternal division; but rather to be taken in this sense, *whatsoever is divided, is divided into such parts as may again be divided;* or thus, *the least divisible thing is not to be given;* or, as geometricians have it, *no quantity is so small, but a less may be taken;* which may easily be demonstrated in this manner. Let any space or time, that which was thought to be the least divisible, be divided into two equal parts, A and B. I say either of them, as A, may be divided again. For suppose the part A to be contiguous to the part B of one side, and of the other side to some other space equal to B. This whole space, therefore, being greater than the

space given, is divisible. Wherefore, if it be divided into two equal parts, the part in the middle, which is A, will be also divided into two equal parts; and therefore A was divisible.

CHAPTER VIII.

OF BODY AND ACCIDENT.

1. Body defined.—2. Accident defined.—3. How an accident may be understood to be in its subject.—4. Magnitude, what it is.—5. Place, what it is, and that it is immovable.—6. What is full and empty.—7. Here, there, somewhere, what they signify.—8. Many bodies cannot be in one place, nor one body in many places.—9. Contiguous and continual, what they are.—10. The definition of motion. No motion intelligible but with time.—11. What it is to be at rest, to have been moved, and to be moved. No motion to be conceived, without the conception of past and future.—12. A point, a line, superfices and solid, what they are.—13. Equal, greater, and less in bodies and magnitudes, what they are.—14. One and the same body has always one and the same magnitude. 15. Velocity, what it is.—16. Equal, greater, and less in times, what they are.—17. Equal, greater, and less, in velocity, what.—18. Equal, greater, and less, in motion, what.—19. That which is at rest, will always be at rest, except it be moved by some external thing; and that which is moved, will always be moved, unless it be hindered by some external thing.—20. Accidents are generated and destroyed, but bodies not so.—21. An accident cannot depart from its subject.—22. Nor be moved.—23. Essence, form, and matter, what they are.—24. First matter, what.—25. That the whole is greater than any part thereof, why demonstrated.

1. HAVING understood what imaginary space is, in which we supposed nothing remaining without us, but all those things to be destroyed, that, by existing heretofore, left images of themselves in our minds; let us

now suppose some one of those things to be placed again in the world, or created anew. It is necessary, therefore, that this new-created or replaced thing do not only fill some part of the space above mentioned, or be coincident and coextended with it, but also that it have no dependance upon our thought. And this is that which, for the extension of it, we commonly call *body;* and because it depends not upon our thought, we say is *a thing subsisting of itself;* as also *existing,* because without us; and, lastly, it is called the *subject,* because it is so placed in and *subjected* to imaginary space, that it may be understood by reason, as well as perceived by sense. The definition, therefore, of *body* may be this, a *body is that, which having no dependance upon our thought, is coincident or coextended with some part of space.*

2. But what an *accident* is cannot so easily be explained by any definition, as by examples. Let us imagine, therefore, that a body fills any space, or is coextended with it; that coextension is not the coextended body: and, in like manner, let us imagine that the same body is removed out of its place; that removing is not the removed body: or let us think the same not removed; that not removing or rest is not the resting body. What, then, are these things? They are *accidents* of that body. But the thing in question is, *what is an accident?* which is an enquiry after that which we know already, and not that which we should enquire after. For who does not always and in the same manner understand him that says any thing is extended, or moved, or not moved? But most men will have it be said that *an accident is something,* namely, some part of a natural thing, when, indeed, it is no part of the same. To satisfy these men, as

well as may be, they answer best that define an *accident* to be *the manner by which any body is conceived;* which is all one as if they should say, *an accident is that faculty of any body, by which it works in us a conception of itself.* Which definition, though it be not an answer to the question propounded, yet it is an answer to that question which should have been propounded, namely, *whence does it happen that one part of any body appears here, another there?* For this is well answered thus: *it happens from the extension of that body.* Or, *how comes it to pass that the whole body, by succession, is seen now here, now there?* and the answer will be, *by reason of its motion.* Or, lastly, *whence is it that any body possesseth the same space for sometime?* and the answer will be, *because it is not moved.* For if concerning the name of a body, that is, concerning a concrete name, it be asked, *what is it?* the answer must be made by definition; for the question is concerning the signification of the name. But if it be asked concerning an abstract name, *what is it?* the cause is demanded why a thing appears so or so. As if it be asked, *what is hard?* The answer will be, hard is that, whereof no part gives place, but when the whole gives place. But if it be demanded, *what is hardness?* a cause must be shewn why a part does not give place, except the whole give place. Wherefore, I define an *accident* to be *the manner of our conception of body.*

3. When an *accident* is said *to be in a body,* it is not so to be understood, as if any thing were contained in that body; as if, for example, redness were in blood, in the same manner, as blood is in a bloody cloth, that is, as a part in the whole; for so, an accident would be a body also. But, as magnitude, or

rest, or motion, is in that which is great, or which resteth, or which is moved, (which, how it is to be understood, every man understands) so also it is to be understood, that every other accident *is in* its subject. And this, also is explicated by *Aristotle* no otherwise than negatively, namely, that *an accident is in its subject, not as any part thereof, but so as that it may be away, the subject still remaining;* which is right, saving that there are certain accidents which can never perish except the body perish also; for no body can be conceived to be without extension, or without figure. All other accidents, which are not common to all bodies, but peculiar to some only, as *to be at rest, to be moved, colour, hardness,* and the like, do perish continually, and are succeeded by others; yet so, as that the body never perisheth. And as for the opinion that some may have, that all other accidents are not in their bodies in the same manner that extension, motion, rest, or figure, are in the same; for example, that colour, heat, odour, virtue, vice, and the like, are otherwise in them, and, as they say, *inherent;* I desire they would suspend their judgment for the present, and expect a little, till it be found out by ratiocination, whether these very accidents are not also certain motions either of the mind of the perceiver, or of the bodies themselves which are perceived; for in the search of this, a great part of natural philosophy consists.

4. The *extension* of a body, is the same thing with the *magnitude* of it, or that which some call *real space.* But this *magnitude* does not depend upon our cogitation, as imaginary space doth; for this is an effect of our imagination, but *magnitude* is the cause of it;

this is an accident of the mind, that of a body existing out of the mind.

5. That space, by which word I here understand imaginary space, which is coincident with the magnitude of any body, is called the *place* of that body; and the body itself is that which we call the *thing placed.* Now *place,* and the *magnitude* of the thing placed, differ. First in this, that a body keeps always the same *magnitude,* both when it is at rest, and when it is moved; but when it is moved, it does not keep the same *place.* Secondly in this, that *place* is a phantasm of any body of such and such quantity and figure; but *magnitude* is the peculiar accident of every body; for one body may at several times have several places, but has always one and the same magnitude. Thirdly in this, that *place* is nothing out of the mind, nor *magnitude* any thing within it. And lastly, *place* is feigned extension, but *magnitude* true extension; and a placed body is not extension, but a thing extended. Besides, *place is immovable;* for, seeing that which is moved, is understood to be carried from place to place, if place were moved, it would also be carried from place to place, so that one place must have another place, and that place another place, and so on infinitely, which is ridiculous. And as for those, that, by making *place* to be of the same nature with *real space,* would from thence maintain it to be immovable, they also make place, though they do not perceive they make it so, to be a mere phantasm. For whilst one affirms that place is therefore said to be immovable, because space in general is considered there; if he had remembered that nothing is general or universal besides names or signs, he would easily have seen that that space, which he says is considered in general, is noth-

ing but a phantasm, in the mind or the memory, of a body of such magnitude and such figure. And whilst another says: real space is made immovable by the understanding; as when, under the superficies of running water, we imagine other and other water to come by continual succession, that superficies fixed there by the understanding, is the *immovable place* of the river: what else does he make it to be but a phantasm, though he do it obscurely and in perplexed words? Lastly, the nature of *place* does not consist in the *superficies of the ambient*, but in *solid space;* for the whole placed body is coextended with its whole place, and every part of it with every answering part of the same place; but seeing every placed body is a solid thing, it cannot be understood to be coextended with superficies. Besides, how can any whole body be moved, unless all its parts be moved together with it? Or how can the internal parts of it be moved, but by leaving their place? But the internal parts of a body cannot leave the superficies of an external part contiguous to it; and, therefore, it follows, that if place be the superficies of the ambient, then the parts of a body moved, that is, bodies moved, are not moved.

6. Space, or place, that is possessed by a body, is called *full*, and that which is not so possessed, is called *empty*.

7. *Here, there, in the country, in the city,* and other the like names, by which answer is made to the question *where is it?* are not properly names of place, nor do they of themselves bring into the mind the place that is sought; for *here* and *there* signify nothing, unless the thing be shewn at the same time with the finger or something else; but when the eye of him

that seeks, is, by pointing or some other sign, directed to the thing sought, the place of it is not hereby defined by him that answers, but found out by him that asks the question. Now such shewings as are made by words only, as when we say, *in the country*, or *in the city*, are some of greater latitude than others, as when we say, *in the country, in the city, in such a street, in a house, in the chamber, in bed*, &c. For these do, by little and little, direct the seeker nearer to the proper place; and yet they do not determine the same, but only restrain it to a lesser space, and signify no more, than that the place of the thing is within a certain space designed by those words, as a part is in the whole. And all such names, by which answer is made to the question *where?* have, for their highest *genus*, the name *somewhere*. From whence it may be understood, that whatsoever is somewhere, is in some place properly so called, which place is part of that greater space that is signified by some of these names, *in the country, in the city*, or the like.

8. A body, and the magnitude, and the place thereof, are divided by one and the same act of the mind; for, to divide an extended body, and the extension thereof, and the idea of that extension, which is place, is the same with dividing any one of them; because they are coincident, and it cannot be done but by mind, that is by the division of space. From whence it is manifest, that neither two bodies can be together in the same place, nor one body be in two places at the same time. Not two bodies in the same place; because when a body that fills its whole place is divided into two, the place itself is divided into two also, so that there will be two places. Not one body in two places; for the place that a body fills being divided into two,

the placed body will be also divided into two; for, as I said, a place and the body that fills that place, are divided both together; and so there will be two bodies.

9. Two bodies are said to be *contiguous* to one another, and *continual*, in the same manner as spaces are; namely, *those are contiguous, between which there is no space.* Now, by space I understand, here as formerly, an idea or phantasm of a body. Wherefore, though between two bodies there be put no other body, and consequently no magnitude, or, as they call it, real space, yet if another body may be put between them, that is, if there intercede any imagined space which may receive another body, then those bodies are not contiguous. And this is so easy to be understood, that I should wonder at some men, who being otherwise skilful enough in philosophy, are of a different opinion, but that I find that most of those that affect metaphysical subtleties wander from truth, as if they were led out of their way by an *ignis fatuus.* For can any man that has his natural senses, think that two bodies must therefore necessarily touch one another, because no other body is between them? Or that there can be no *vacuum*, because *vacuum* is nothing, or as they call it, *non ens?* Which is as childish, as if one should reason thus; no man can fast, because to fast is to eat nothing; but nothing cannot be eaten. *Continual, are any two bodies that have a common part; and more than two are continual, when every two, that are next to one another, are continual.*

10. MOTION *is a continual relinquishing of one place, and acquiring of another;* and that place which is relinquished is commonly called the *terminus a quo,* as that which is acquired is called the *terminus ad quem;* I say a continual relinquishing, because no body,

how little soever, can totally and at once go out of its former place into another, so, but that some part of it will be in a part of a place which is common to both, namely, to the relinquished and the acquired places.

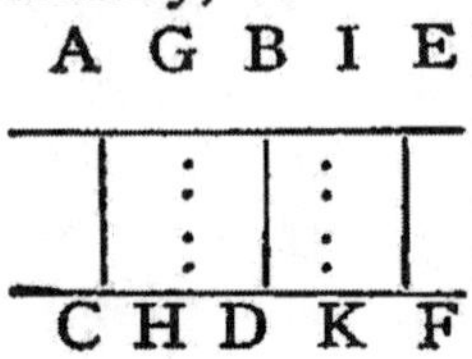

For example, let any body be in the place A C B D; the same body cannot come into the place B D E F, but it must first be in G H I K, whose part G H B D is common to both the places A C B D, and G H I K, and whose part B D I K, is common to both the places G H I K, and B D E F. Now it cannot be conceived that anything can be moved without time; for time is, by the definition of it, a phantasm, that is, a conception of motion; and, therefore, to conceive that any thing may be moved without time, were to conceive motion without motion, which is impossible.

11. *That is said to be at rest, which, during any time, is in one place; and that to be moved, or to have been moved, which, whether it be now at rest or moved, was formerly in another place than that which it is now in.* From which definitions it may be inferred, first, that *whatsoever is moved, has been moved;* for if it be still in the same place in which it was formerly, it is at rest, that is, it is not moved, by the definition of *rest;* but if it be in another place, it has been moved, by the definition of *moved.* Secondly, that *what is moved, will yet be moved;* for that which is moved, leaveth the place where it is, and therefore will be in another place, and consequently will be moved still. Thirdly, that *whatsoever is moved, is not in one place during any time, how little soever that time be;* for by the definition of rest, that which is in one place during any time, is at rest.

There is a certain sophism against motion, which seems to spring from the not understanding of this last proposition. For they say, that, *if any body be moved, it is moved either in the place where it is, or in the place where it is not; both which are false; and therefore nothing is moved.* But the falsity lies in the major proposition; for that which is moved, is neither moved in the place where it is, nor in the place where it is not; but from the place where it is, to the place where it is not. Indeed it cannot be denied but that whatsoever is moved, is moved somewhere, that is, within some space; but then the place of that body is not that whole space, but a part of it, as is said above in the seventh article. From what is above demonstrated, namely, that whatsoever is moved, has also been moved, and will be moved, this also may be collected, that there can be no conception of motion, without conceiving past and future time.

12. Though there be no body which has not some magnitude, yet if, when any body is moved, the magnitude of it be not at all considered, the way it makes is called a *line,* or one single dimension; and the space, through which it passeth, is called *length;* and the body itself, a *point;* in which sense the earth is called a *point,* and the way of its yearly revolution, the *ecliptic line.* But if a body, which is moved, be considered as *long,* and be supposed to be so moved, as that all the several parts of it be understood to make several lines, then the way of every part of that body is called *breadth,* and the space which is made is called *superficies,* consisting of two dimensions, one whereof to every several part of the other is applied whole. Again, if a body be considered as having *superficies,* and be understood to be so moved, that all the several

parts of it describe several lines, then the way of every part of that body is called *thickness* or *depth*, and the space which is made is called solid, consisting of three dimensions, any two whereof are applied whole to every several part of the third.

But if a body be considered as *solid*, then it is not possible that all the several parts of it should describe several lines; for what way soever it be moved, the way of the following part will fall into the way of the part before it, so that the same solid will still be made which the foremost superficies would have made by itself. And therefore there can be no other dimension in any body, as it is a body, than the three which I have now described; though, as it shall be shewed hereafter, *velocity*, which is motion according to *length*, may, by being applied to all the parts of a *solid*, make a magnitude of motion, consisting of four dimensions; as the goodness of gold, computed in all the parts of it, makes the price and value thereof.

13. *Bodies*, how many soever they be, that can fill every one the place of every one, are said to be *equal* every one to every other. Now, one body may fill the same place which another body filleth, though it be not of the same figure with that other body, if so be that it may be understood to be reducible to the same figure, either by flexion or transposition of the parts. And *one body is greater than another body, when a part of that is equal to all this; and less, when all that is equal to a part of this.* Also, *magnitudes* are *equal*, or *greater*, or *lesser*, than one another, for the same consideration, namely, when the bodies, of which they are the magnitudes, are either *equal*, or *greater*, or *less*, &c.

14. One and the same body is always of one and

the same magnitude. For seeing a body and the magnitude and place thereof cannot be comprehended in the mind otherwise than as they are coincident, if any body be understood to be at rest, that is, to remain in the same place during some time, and the magnitude thereof be in one part of that time greater, and in another part less, that body's place, which is one and the same, will be coincident sometimes with greater, sometimes with less magnitude, that is, the same place will be greater and less than itself, which is impossible. But there would be no need at all of demonstrating a thing that is in itself so manifest, if there were not some, whose opinion concerning bodies and their magnitudes is, that a body may exist separated from its magnitude, and have greater or less magnitude bestowed upon it, making use of this principle for the explication of the nature of *rarum* and *densum*.

15. Motion, in as much as a certain length may in a certain time be transmitted by it, is called VELOCITY or *swiftness:* &c. For though *swift* be very often understood with relation to *slower* or *less swift,* as great is in respect of less, yet nevertheless, as magnitude is by philosophers taken absolutely for extension, so also *velocity* or *swiftness* may be put absolutely for motion according to length.

16. Many motions are said to be made in equal times, when every one of them begins and ends together with some other motion, or if it had begun together, would also have ended together with the same. For time, which is a phantasm of motion, cannot be reckoned but by some exposed motion; as in dials by the motion of the sun or of the hand; and if two or more motions begin and end with this motion, they are said to be made in equal times; from whence

also it is easy to understand what it is to be moved in greater or longer time, and in less time or not so long; namely, that that is longer moved, which beginning with another, ends later; or ending together, began sooner.

17. Motions are said to be equally swift, when equal lengths are transmitted in equal times; and greater swiftness is that, wherein greater length is passed in equal time, or equal length in less time. Also that swiftness by which equal lengths are passed in equal parts of time, is called *uniform* swiftness or motion; and of motions *not uniform*, such as become swifter or slower by equal increasings or decreasings in equal parts of time, are said to be *accelerated* or *retarded uniformly*.

18. But motion is said to be greater, less, and equal, not only in regard of the length which is transmitted in a certain time, that is, in regard of swiftness only, but of swiftness applied to every smallest particle of magnitude; for when any body is moved, every part of it is also moved; and supposing the parts to be halves, the motions of those halves have their swiftness equal to one another, and severally equal to that of the whole; but the motion of the whole is equal to those two motions, either of which is of equal swiftness with it; and therefore it is one thing for two motions to be equal to one another, and another thing for them to be equally swift. And this is manifest in two horses that draw abreast, where the motion of both the horses together is of equal swiftness with the motion of either of them singly; but the motion of both is greater than the motion of one of them, namely, double. Wherefore *motions are said to be simply equal to one another, when the swiftness of one, computed in every part of*

its magnitude, is equal to the swiftness of the other computed also in every part of its magnitude: and greater than one another, when the swiftness of one computed as above, is greater than the swiftness of the other so computed; and less, when less. Besides, the magnitude of motion computed in this manner is that which is commonly called FORCE.

19. *Whatsoever is at rest, will always be at rest, unless there be some other body besides it, which, by endeavoring to get into its place by motion, suffers it no longer to remain at rest.* For suppose that some finite body exist and be at rest, and that all space besides be empty; if now this body begin to be moved, it will certainly be moved some way; seeing therefore there was nothing in that body which did not dispose it to rest, the reason why it is moved this way is in something out of it; and in like manner, if it had been moved any other way, the reason of motion that way had also been in something out of it; but seeing it was supposed that nothing is out of it, the reason of its motion one way would be the same with the reason of its motion every other way, wherefore it would be moved alike all ways at once; which is impossible.

In like manner, *whatsoever is moved, will always be moved, except there be some other body besides it, which causeth it to rest.* For if we suppose nothing to be without it, there will be no reason why it should rest now, rather than at another time; wherefore its motion would cease in every particle of time alike; which is not intelligible.

20. When we say a living creature, a tree, or any other specified body is *generated* or *destroyed,* it is not to be so understood as if there were made a body of that which is not-body, or not a body of a body, but of a

living creature not a living creature, of a tree not a tree, &c. that is, that those accidents for which we call one thing a living creature, another thing a tree, and another by some other name, are generated and destroyed; and that therefore the same names are not to be given to them now, which were given them before. But that magnitude for which we give to any thing the name of body is neither generated nor destroyed. For though we may feign in our mind that a point may swell to a huge bulk, and that this may again contract itself to a point; that is, though we may imagine something to rise where before was nothing, and nothing to be there where before was something, yet we cannot comprehend in our mind how this may possibly be done in nature. And therefore philosophers, who tie themselves to natural reason, suppose that a body can neither be generated nor destroyed, but only that it may appear otherwise than it did to us, that is, under different *species*, and consequently be called by other and other names; so that that which is now called man, may at another time have the name of not-man; but that which is once called body, can never be called not-body. But it is manifest, that all other accidents besides magnitude or extension may be generated and destroyed; as when a white thing is made black, the whiteness that was in it perisheth, and the blackness that was not in it is now generated; and therefore bodies, and the accidents under which they appear diversely, have this difference, that bodies are things, and not generated; accidents are generated, and not things.

21. And therefore, when any thing appears otherwise than it did by reason of other and other accidents, it is not to be thought that an accident goes out

of one subject into another, (for they are not, as I said above, in their subjects as a part in the whole, or as a contained thing in that which contains it, or as a master of a family in his house,) but that one accident perisheth, and another is generated. For example, when the hand, being moved, moves the pen, motion does not go out of the hand into the pen; for so the writing might be continued though the hand stood still; but a new motion is generated in the pen, and is the pen's motion.

22. And therefore also it is improper to say, an accident is moved; as when, instead of saying, *figure is an accident of a body carried away*, we say, *a body carries away its figure.*

23. Now that accident for which we give a certain name to any body, or the accident which denominates its subject, is commonly called the ESSENCE thereof; as rationality is the essence of a man; whiteness, of any white thing, and extension the essence of a body. And the same essence, in as much as it is generated, is called the FORM. Again, a body, in respect of any accident, is called the SUBJECT, and in respect of the form it is called the MATTER.

Also, the production or perishing of any accident makes its subject be said *to be changed;* only the production or perishing of form makes it be said it is *generated* or *destroyed;* but in all generation and mutation, the name of *matter* still remains. For a table made of wood is not only wooden, but wood; and a statue of brass is brass as well as brazen; though Aristotle, in his *Metaphysics,* says that whatsoever is made of any thing ought not to be called ἐκεινὸ; but ἐκείνινον; as that which is made of wood, not ξύλον but ξύλινον, that is, not wood, but wooden.

24. And as for that matter which is common to all things, and which philosophers, following Aristotle, usually call *materia prima,* that is, *first matter,* it is not any body distinct from all other bodies, nor is it one of them. What then is it? A mere name; yet a name which is not of vain use; for it signifies a conception of body without the consideration of any form or other accident except only magnitude or extension, and aptness to receive form and other accident. So that whensoever we have use of the name *body in general,* if we use that of *materia prima,* we do well. For as when a man not knowing which was first, water or ice, would find out which of the two were the matter of both, he would be fain to suppose some third matter which were neither of these two; so he that would find out what is the matter of all things, ought to suppose such as is not the matter of anything that exists. Wherefore *materia prima* is nothing; and therefore they do not attribute to it either form or any other accident besides quantity; whereas all singular things have their forms and accidents certain.

Materia prima, therefore, is body in general, that is, body considered universally, not as having neither form nor any accident, but in which no form nor any other accident but quantity are at all considered, that is, they are not drawn into argumentation.

25. From what has been said, those axioms may be demonstrated, which are assumed by Euclid in the beginning of his first element, about the equality and inequality of magnitudes; of which, omitting the rest, I will here demonstrate only this one, *the whole is greater than any part thereof;* to the end that the reader may know that those axioms are not indemonstrable, and therefore not principles of demonstration;

and from hence learn to be wary how he admits any thing for a principle, which is not at least as evident as these are. *Greater* is defined to be that, whose part is equal to the whole of another. Now if we suppose any whole to be A, and a part of it to be B; seeing the whole B is equal to itself, and the same B is a part of A; therefore a part of A will be equal to the whole B. Wherefore, by the definition above, A is greater than B; which was to be proved.

CHAPTER IX.

OF CAUSE AND EFFECT.

1. Action and passion, what they are.—2. Action and passion mediate and immediate.—3. Cause simply taken. Cause without which no effect follows, or cause necessary by supposition.—4. Cause efficient and material.—5. An entire cause is always sufficient to produce its effect. At the same instant that the cause is entire, the effect is produced. Every effect has a necessary cause.—6. The generation of effects is continual. What is the beginning in causation.—7. No cause of motion but in a body contiguous and moved.—8. The same agents and patients, if alike disposed, produce like effects though at different times.—9. All mutation is motion.—10. Contingent accidents, what they are.

1. A BODY is said to work upon or *act*, that is to say, *do* something to another body, when it either generates or destroys some accident in it: and the body in which an accident is generated or destroyed is said to *suffer*, that is, to have something *done* to it by another body; as when one body by putting forwards another body generates motion in it, it is called the AGENT; and the body in which motion is so generated, is called the PATIENT; so fire that warms the hand is the *agent*, and

the hand, which is warmed, is the *patient*. That accident, which is generated in the patient, is called the EFFECT.

2. When an agent and patient are contiguous to one another, their action and passion are then said to be *immediate*, otherwise, *mediate;* and when another body, lying betwixt the agent and patient, is contiguous to them both, it is then itself both an agent and a patient; an agent in respect of the body next after it, upon which it works, and a patient in respect of the body next before it, from which it suffers. Also, if many bodies be so ordered that every two which are next to one another be contiguous, then all those that are betwixt the first and the last are both agents and patients, and the first is an agent only, and the last a patient only.

3. An agent is understood to *produce* its determined or certain effect in the patient, according to some certain accident or accidents, with which both it and the patient are affected; that is to say, the agent hath its effect precisely such, not because it is a body, but because such a body, or so moved. For otherwise all agents, seeing they are all bodies alike, would produce like effects in all patients. And therefore the fire, for example, does not warm, because it is a body, but because it is hot; nor does one body put forward another body because it is a body, but because it is moved into the place of that other body. The cause, therefore, of all effects consists in certain accidents both in the agents and in the patients; which when they are all present, the effect is produced; but if any one of them be wanting, it is not produced; and that accident either of the agent or patient, without which the effect cannot be produced, is called *causa sine qua*

non, or *cause necessary by supposition,* as also the *cause requisite for the production of the effect.* But a CAUSE simply, or *an entire cause, is the aggregate of all the accidents both of the agents how many soever they be, and of the patient, put together; which when they are all supposed to be present, it cannot be understood but that the effect is produced at the same instant; and if any one of them be wanting, it cannot be understood but that the effect is not produced.*

4. The aggregate of accidents in the agent or agents, requisite for the production of the effect, the effect being produced, is called the *efficient cause* thereof; and the aggregate of accidents in the patient, the effect being produced, is usually called the *material cause;* I say the effect being produced; for where there is no effect there can be no cause; for nothing can be called a cause, where there is nothing that can be called an effect. But the efficient and material causes are both but partial causes, or parts of that cause, which in the next precedent article I called an entire cause. And from hence it is manifest, that the effect we expect, though the agents be not defective on their part, may nevertheless be frustrated by a defect in the patient; and when the patient is sufficient, by a defect in the agents.

5. An entire cause is always sufficient for the production of its effect, if the effect be at all possible. For let any effect whatsoever be propounded to be produced; if the same be produced, it is manifest that the cause which produced it was a sufficient cause; but if it be not produced, and yet be possible, it is evident that something was wanting either in some agent, or in the patient, without which it could not be produced; that is, that some accident was wanting which was

requisite for its production; and therefore, that cause was not *entire*, which is contrary to what was supposed.

It follows also from hence, that in whatsoever instant the cause is entire, in the same instant the effect is produced. For if it be not produced, something is still wanting, which is requisite for the production of it; and therefore the cause was not entire, as was supposed.

And seeing a necessary cause is defined to be that, which being supposed, the effect cannot but follow; this also may be collected, that whatsoever effect is produced at any time, the same is produced by a necessary cause. For whatsoever is produced, in as much as it is produced, had an entire cause, that is, had all those things, which being supposed, it cannot be understood but that the effect follows; that is, it had a necessary cause. And in the same manner it may be shewn, that whatsoever effects are hereafter to be produced, shall have a necessary cause; so that all the effects that have been, or shall be produced, have their necessity in things antecedent.

6. And from this, that whensoever the cause is entire, the effect is produced in the same instant, it is manifest that causation and the production of effects consist in a certain continual progress; so that as there is a continual mutation in the agent or agents, by the working of other agents upon them, so also the patient, upon which they work, is continually altered and changed. For example: as the heat of the fire increases more and more, so also the effects thereof, namely, the heat of such bodies as are next to it, and again, of such other bodies as are next to them, increase more and more accordingly; which is already no little

argument that all mutation consists in motion only; the truth whereof shall be further demonstrated in the ninth article. But in this progress of causation, that is, of action and passion, if any man comprehend in his imagination a part thereof, and divide the same into parts, the first part or beginning of it cannot be considered otherwise than as action or cause; for, if it should be considered as effect or passion, then it would be necessary to consider something before it, for its cause or action; which cannot be, for nothing can be before the beginning. And in like manner, the last part is considered only as effect; for it cannot be called cause, if nothing follow it; but after the last, nothing follows. And from hence it is, that in all action the beginning and cause are taken for the same thing. But every one of the intermediate parts are both action and passion, and cause and effect, according as they are compared with the antecedent or subsequent part.

7. There can be no cause of motion, except in a body contiguous and moved. For let there be any two bodies which are not contiguous, and betwixt which the intermediate space is empty, or, if filled, filled with another body which is at rest; and let one of the propounded bodies be supposed to be at rest; I say it shall always be at rest. For it if shall be moved, the cause of that motion, by the 8th chapter, article 19, will be some external body; and, therefore, if between it and that external body there be nothing but empty space, then whatsoever the disposition be of that external body or of the patient itself, yet if it be supposed to be now at rest, we may conceive it will continue so till it be touched by some other body. But seeing cause, by

the definition, is the aggregate of all such accidents, which being supposed to be present, it cannot be conceived but that the effect will follow, those accidents, which are either in external bodies, or in the patient itself, cannot be the cause of future motion. And in like manner, seeing we may conceive that whatsoever is at rest will still be at rest, though it be touched by some other body, except that other body be moved; therefore in a contiguous body, which is at rest, there can be no cause of motion. Wherefore there is no cause of motion in any body, except it be contiguous and moved.

The same reason may serve to prove that whatsoever is moved, will always be moved on in the same way and with the same velocity, except it be hindered by some other contiguous and moved body; and consequently that no bodies, either when they are at rest, or when there is an interposition of vacuum, can generate or extinguish or lessen motion in other bodies. There is one that has written that things moved are more resisted by things at rest, than by things contrarily moved; for this reason, that he conceived motion not to be so contrary to motion as rest. That which deceived him was, that the words *rest* and *motion* are but contradictory names; whereas motion, indeed, is not resisted by rest, but by contrary motion.

8. But if a body work upon another body at one time, and afterwards the same body work upon the same body at another time, so that both the agent and patient, and all their parts, be in all things as they were; and there be no difference, except only in time, that is, that one action be former, the other later in time; it is manifest of itself, that the effects will be equal and like, as not differing in anything besides time. And

as effects themselves proceed from their causes, so the diversity of them depends upon the diversity of their causes also.

9. This being true, it is necessary that mutation can be nothing else but motion of the parts of that body which is changed. For first, we do not say anything is changed, but that which appears to our senses otherwise than it appeared formerly. Secondly, both those appearances are effects produced in the sentient; and, therefore, if they be different, it is necessary, by the preceding article, that either some part of the agent, which was formerly at rest, is now moved, and so the mutation consists in this motion; or some part, which was formerly moved, is now otherwise moved, and so also the mutation consists in this new motion; or which, being formerly moved, is now at rest, which, as I have shewn above, cannot come to pass without motion; and so again, mutation is motion; or lastly, it happens in some of these manners to the patient, or some of its parts; so that mutation, howsoever it be made, will consist in the motion of the parts, either of the body which is perceived, or of the sentient body, or of both. Mutation therefore is motion, namely, of the parts either of the agent or of the patient; which was to be demonstrated. And to this it is consequent, that rest cannot be the cause of anything, nor can any action proceed from it; seeing neither motion nor mutation can be caused by it.

10. Accidents, in respect of other accidents which precede them, or are before them in time, and upon which they do not depend as upon their causes, are called *contingent* accidents; I say, in respect of those accidents by which they are not generated; for, in respect of their causes, all things come to pass with

equal necessity; for otherwise they would have no causes at all; which, of things generated, is not intelligible.

CHAPTER X.

OF POWER AND ACT.

1. Power and cause are the same thing.—2. An act is produced at the same instant in which the power is plenary.—3. Active and passive power are parts only of plenary power.—4. An act, when said to be possible.—5. An act necessary and contingent, what.—6. Active power consists in motion.—7. Cause, formal and final, what they are.

1. CORRESPONDENT to *cause* and *effect*, are POWER and ACT; nay, those and these are the same things; though, for divers considerations, they have divers names. For whensoever any agent has all those accidents which are necessarily requisite for the production of some effect in the patient, then we say that agent has *power* to produce that effect, if it be applied to a patient. But, as I have shewn in the precedent chapter, those accidents constitute the efficient cause; and therefore the same accidents, which constitute the efficient cause, constitute also the *power* of the agent. Wherefore the *power of the agent* and the *efficient cause* are the same thing. But they are considered with this difference, that *cause* is so called in respect to the effect already produced, and power in respect of the same effect to be produced hereafter; so that *cause* respects the past, *power* the future time. Also, the *power of the agent* is that which is commonly called *active power*.

In like manner, whensoever any patient has all those

accidents which it is requisite it should have, for the production of some effect in it, we say it is in the *power* of that patient to produce that effect, if it be applied to a fitting agent. But those accidents, as is defined in the precedent chapter, constitute the material cause; and therefore the *power of the patient,* commonly called *passive power,* and *material cause,* are the same thing; but with this different consideration, that in cause the past time, and in power the future, is respected. Wherefore the power of the agent and patient together, which may be called entire or *plenary power,* is the same thing with *entire cause;* for they both consist in the sum or aggregate of all the accidents, as well in the agent as in the patient, which are requisite for the production of the effect. Lastly, as the accident produced is, in respect of the cause, called an effect, so in respect of the power, it is called an *act.*

2. As therefore the effect is produced in the same instant in which the cause is entire, so also every act that may be produced, is produced in the same instant in which the power is plenary. And as there can be no effect but from a sufficient and necessary cause, so also no act can be produced but by sufficient power, or that power by which it could not but be produced.

3. And as it is manifest, as I have shewn, that the efficient and material causes are severally and by themselves parts only of an entire cause, and cannot produce any effect but by being joined together, so also power, active and passive, are parts only of plenary and entire power; nor, except they be joined, can any act proceed from them; and therefore these powers, as I said in the first article, are but conditional, namely, *the agent has power, if it be applied to a patient; and the patient has power, if it be applied to an agent;* otherwise

neither of them have power, nor can the accidents, which are in them severally, be properly called powers; nor any action be said to be possible for the power of the agent alone or of the patient alone.

4. For that is an impossible act, for the production of which there is no power plenary. For seeing plenary power is that in which all things concur, which are requisite for the production of an act, if the power shall never be plenary, there will always be wanting some of those things, without which the act cannot be produced; wherefore that act shall never be produced; that is, that act is IMPOSSIBLE: and every act, which is not impossible, is POSSIBLE. Every act, therefore, which is possible, shall at some time be produced; for if it shall never be produced, then those things shall never concur which are requisite for the production of it; wherefore that act is *impossible*, by the definition; which is contrary to what was supposed.

5. A *necessary act* is that, the production whereof it is impossible to hinder; and therefore every act, that shall be produced, shall necessarily be produced; for, that it shall not be produced, is impossible; because, as is already demonstrated, every possible act shall at some time be produced; nay, this proposition, *what shall be, shall be,* is as necessary a proposition as this, *a man is a man.*

But here, perhaps, some man may ask whether those future things, which are commonly called *contingents,* are necessary. I say, therefore, that generally all contingents have their necessary causes, as is shewn in the preceding chapter; but are called contingents in respect of other events, upon which they do not depend; as the rain, which shall be tomorrow, shall be necessary, that is, from necessary causes; but we think and say it happens by chance, because we do not yet perceive the causes thereof, though they exist now; for men commonly call that *casual* or *contingent,* whereof they do not perceive the necessary cause; and in the same manner they used to speak of things past, when not knowing whether a thing be done or no, they say it is possible it never was done.

Wherefore, all propositions concerning future things, contingent or not contingent, as this, *it will rain tomorrow,* or this, *tomorrow the sun will rise,* are either necessarily true, or necessarily false; but we call them contingent because we do not yet know whether they be true or false; whereas their verity depends not upon our knowledge, but upon the foregoing of their causes. But there are some, who though they confess this whole proposition, *tomorrow it will either rain, or not rain,* to be true, yet they will not acknowledge the parts of it, as, *tomorrow it will rain,* or, *tomorrow it will not rain,* to be either of them true by itself; because they say neither this nor that is true *determinately.* But what is this *determinately true,* but true upon our knowledge, or evidently true? And therefore they say no more but that it is not yet known whether it be true or no; but they say it more obscurely, and darken the evidence of the truth with the same words, with which they endeavour to hide their own ignorance.

6. In the 9th article of the preceding chapter, I have shewn that the efficient cause of all motion and mutation consists in the motion of the agent, or agents; and in the first article of this chapter, that the power of the agent is the same thing with the efficient cause. From whence it may be understood, that all active power consists in motion also; and that power is not a

certain accident, which differs from all acts, but is, indeed, an act, namely, motion, which is therefore called power, because another act shall be produced by it afterwards. For example, if of three bodies the first put forward the second, and this the third, the motion of the second, in respect of the first which produceth it, is the act of the second body; but, in respect of the third, it is the active power of the same second body.

7. The writers of metaphysics reckon up two other causes besides the *efficient* and *material*, namely, the ESSENCE, which some call the *formal cause*, and the END, or *final cause;* both which are nevertheless efficient causes. For when it is said the essence of a thing is the cause thereof, *as to be rational is the cause of man*, it is not intelligible; for it is all one, as if it were said, *to be a man is the cause of man;* which is not well said. And yet the knowledge of the *essence* of anything, is the cause of the knowledge of the thing itself; for, if I first know that a thing is *rational*, I know from thence, that the same is *man;* but this is no other than an efficient cause. A *final cause* has no place but in such things as have sense and will; and this also I shall prove hereafter to be an efficient cause.

CHAPTER XI.

OF IDENTITY AND DIFFERENCE.

1. What it is for one thing to differ from another.—2. To differ in number, magnitude, species, and genus, what.—3. What is relation, proportion, and relatives.—4. Proportionals, what.—5. The proportion of magnitudes to one another, wherein it consists.—6. Relation is no new accident, but one of those that were in the relative before the relation or comparison was made. Also the causes of accidents in the

correlatives, are the cause of relation.—7. Of the beginning of individuation.

1. HITHERTO I have spoken of body simply, and accidents common to all bodies, as *magnitude, motion, rest, action, passion, power, possible,* &c.; and I should now descend to those accidents by which one body is distinguished from another but that it is first to be declared what it is to be *distinct* and *not distinct,* namely, what are the SAME and DIFFERENT; for this also is common to all bodies, that they may be distinguished and differenced from one another. Now, two bodies are said to *differ* from one another, when something may be said of one of them, which cannot be said of the other at the same time.

2. And, first of all, it is manifest that no two bodies are the *same;* for seeing they are two, they are in two places at the same time; as that, which is the *same,* is at the same time in one and the same place. All bodies therefore differ from one another in *number,* namely, as one another; so that the *same* and *different in number,* are names opposed to one another by contradiction.

In *magnitude* bodies differ when one is greater than another, as *a cubit long,* and *two cubits long,* of *two pound weight,* and of *three pound weight.* And to these, *equals* are opposed.

Bodies which differ more than in magnitude, are called *unlike;* and those, which differ only in magnitude, *like.* Also, of unlike bodies, some are said to differ in the *species,* other in the *genus;* in the *species,* when their difference is perceived by one and the same sense, as *white* and *black;* and in the *genus,* when their difference is not perceived but by divers senses, as *white* and *hot*.

3. And the *likeness,* or *unlikeness, equality,* or *inequality* of one body to another, is called their RELATION; and the bodies themselves *relatives* or *correlatives; Aristotle* calls them τά πρὸς τὶ; the first whereof is usually named the *antecedent,* and the second the *consequent;* and the *relation* of the antecedent to the consequent, according to magnitude, namely, the equality, the excess or defect thereof, is called the PROPORTION of the antecedent to the consequent; so that *proportion* is nothing but the equality or inequality of the magnitude of the antecedent compared to the magnitude of the consequent by their difference only, or compared also with their difference. For example, the *proportion* of three to two consists only in this, that three *exceeds* two by unity; and the proportion of two to five in this, that two, compared with five, is *deficient* of it by three, either simply, or compared with the numbers different; and therefore in the proportion of unequals, the proportion of the less to the greater, is called DEFECT; and that of the greater to the less, EXCESS.

4. Besides, of unequals, some are more, some less, and some equally unequal; so that there is *proportion of proportions,* as well as of *magnitudes;* namely, where two unequals have relation to two other unequals; as, when the inequality which is between 2 and 3, is compared with the inequality which is between 4 and 5. In which comparison there are always four magnitudes; or, which is all one, if there be but three, the middle most is twice numbered; and if the proportion of the first to the second, be equal to the proportion of the third to the fourth, then the four are said

to be *proportionals;* otherwise they are not proportionals.

5. The proportion of the antecendent to the consequent consists in their difference, not only simply taken, but also as compared with one of the relatives; that is, either in that part of the greater, by which it exceeds the less, or in the remainder, after the less is taken out of the greater; as the proportion of two to five consists in the three by which five exceeds two, not in three simply only, but also as compared with five or two. For though there be the same difference between two and five, which is between nine and twelve, namely three, yet there is not the same inequality; and therefore the proportion of two to five is not in all relation the same with that of nine to twelve, but only in that which is called arithmetical.

6. But we must not so think of relation, as if it were an accident differing from all the other accidents of the relative; but one of them, namely, that by which the comparison is made. For example, the likeness of one *white* to another *white,* or its unlikeness to *black,* is the same accident with its *whiteness;* and *equality* and *inequality,* the same accident with the *magnitude* of the thing compared, though under another name: for that which is called *white* or *great,* when it is not compared with something else, the same when it is compared, is called *like* or *unlike, equal* or *unequal.* And from this it follows that the causes of the accidents, which are in relatives, are the causes also of *likeness, unlikeness, equality* and *inequality;* namely, that he, that makes two unequal bodies, makes also their inequality; and he, that makes a rule and an action, makes also, if the action be congruous to the rule, their congruity; if incongruous, their incongru-

ity. And thus much concerning *comparison* of one body with another.

7. But the same body may at different times be compared with itself. And from hence springs a great controversy among philosophers about the *beginning of individuation,* namely, in what sense it may be conceived that a body is at one time the same, at another time not the same it was formerly. For example, whether a man grown old be the same man he was whilst he was young, or another man; or whether a city be in different ages the same, or another city. Some place *individuity* in the unity of *matter;* others in the unity of *form;* and one says it consists in the unity of the *aggregate of all the accidents together.* For *matter,* it is pleaded that a lump of wax, whether it be spherical or cubical, is the same wax, because the same matter. For *form,* that when a man is grown from an infant to be an old man, though his matter be changed, yet he is still the same numerical man; for that *identity,* which cannot be attributed to the matter, ought probably to be ascribed to the form. For the *aggregate of accidents,* no instance can be made; but because, when any new accident is generated, a new name is commonly imposed on the thing, therefore he, that assigned this cause of *individuity,* thought the thing itself also was become another thing. According to the first opinion, he that sins, and he that is punished, should not be the same man, by reason of the perpetual flux and change of man's body; nor should the city, which makes laws in one age and abrogates them in another, be the same city; which were to confound all civil rights. According to the second opinion, two bodies existing both at once, would be one and the same numerical body. For if,

for example, that ship of Theseus, concerning the difference whereof made by continual reparation in taking out the old planks and putting in new, the sophisters of Athens were wont to dispute, were, after all the planks were changed, the same numerical ship it was at the beginning; and if some man had kept the old planks as they were taken out, and by putting them afterwards together in the same order, had again made a ship of them, this, without doubt, had also been the same numerical ship with that which was at the beginning; and so there would have been two ships numerically the same, which is absurd. But, according to the third opinion, nothing would be the same it was; so that a man standing would not be the same he was sitting; nor the water, which is in the vessel, the same with that which is poured out of it. Wherefore the beginning of *individuation* is not always to be taken either from matter alone, or from form alone.

But we must consider by what name anything is called, when we inquire concerning the *identity* of it. For it is one thing to ask concerning Socrates, whether he be the same man, and another to ask whether he be the same body; for his body, when he is old, cannot be the same it was when he was an infant, by reason of the difference of magnitude; for one body has always one and the same magnitude; yet, nevertheless, he may be the same man. And therefore, whensoever the name, by which it is asked whether a thing be the same it was, is given it for the matter only, then, if the matter be the same, the thing also is *individually* the same; as the water, which was in the sea, is the same which is afterwards in the cloud; and any body is the same, whether the parts of it be put together, or dispersed; or whether it be congealed, or dissolved. Also, if the name be given for such form as is the beginning of motion, then, as long as that motion remains, it will be the same *individual* thing; as that man will be always the same, whose actions and thoughts proceed all from the same beginning of motion, namely, that which was in his generation; and that will be the same river which flows from one and the same fountain, whether the same water, or other water, or something else than water, flow from thence; and that the same city, whose acts proceed continually from the same institution, whether the men be the same or no. Lastly, if the name be given for some accident, then the *identity* of the thing will depend upon the matter; for, by the taking away and supplying of matter, the accidents that were, are destroyed, and other new ones are generated, which cannot be the same numerically; so that a ship, which signifies matter so figured, will be the same as long as the matter remains the same; but if no part of the matter be the same, then it is numerically another ship; and if part of the matter remain and part be changed, then the ship will be partly the same, and partly not the same.

CHAPTER XII*.

OF QUANTITY.

1. The definition of quantity.—2. The exposition of quantity, what it is.—3. How line, superficies, and solid are exposed. 4. How time is exposed.—5. How number is exposed.—6.

---

* For list of the writings of Hobbes on mathematics, cf. p. xviii.

How velocity is exposed.—7. How weight is exposed.—8 How the proportion of magnitudes is exposed.—9. How the proportion of times and velocities is exposed.

1. WHAT and how manifold *dimension* is, has been said in the 8th chapter, namely, that there are three dimensions, line or length, superficies, and solid; every one of which, if it be determined, that is, if the limits of it be made known, is commonly called *quantity;* for by *quantity* all men understand that which is signified by that word, by which answer is made to the question, *How much is it?* Whensoever, therefore, it is asked, for example, *How long is the journey?* it is not answered indefinitely, *length;* nor, when it is asked, *How big is the field?* is it answered indefinitely, *superficies;* nor, if a man ask, *How great is the bulk?* indefinitely, *solid:* but it is answered determinately, the journey is a hundred miles; the field is a hundred acres; the bulk is a hundred cubical feet; or at least in some such manner, that the magnitude of the thing enquired after may by certain limits be comprehended in the mind. QUANTITY, therefore, cannot otherwise be defined, than to be *a dimension determined,* or *a dimension, whose limits are set out, either by their place, or by some comparison.*

2. And *quantity* is determined two ways; one, by the sense, when some sensible object is set before it; as when a line, a superficies or solid, of a foot or cubit, marked out in some matter, is objected to the eyes; which way of determining, is called *exposition,* and the quantity so known is called *exposed quantity;* the other by memory, that is, by comparison with some exposed quantity. In the first manner, when it is asked of what quantity a thing is, it is answered,

of such quantity as you see exposed. In the second manner, answer cannot be made but by comparison with some exposed quantity; for if it be asked, how long is the way? the answer is, so many thousand paces; that is, by comparing the way with a pace, or some other measure, determined and known by exposition; or the quantity of it is to some other quantity known by exposition, as the diameter of a square is to the side of the same, or by some other the like means. But it is to be understood, that the quantity exposed must be some standing or permanent thing, such as is marked out in consistent or durable matter; or at least something which is revocable to sense; for otherwise no comparison can be made by it. Seeing, therefore, by what has been said in the next preceding chapter, comparison of one magnitude with another is the same thing with proportion; it is manifest, that quantity determined in the second manner is nothing else but the proportion of a dimension not exposed to another which is exposed; that is, the comparison of the equality or inequality thereof with an exposed quantity.

3. *Lines, superficies,* and *solids,* are exposed, first, by *motion,* in such manner as in the 8th chapter I have said they are generated; but so as that the marks of such motion be permanent; as when they are designed upon some matter, as a line upon paper; or graven in some durable matter. Secondly, by *apposition;* as when one line or length is applied to another line or length, one breadth to another breadth, and one thickness to another thickness; which is as much as to describe a line by points, a superficies by lines, and a solid by superficies; saving that by points in this place are to be understood very short lines; and, by

superficies, very thin solids. Thirdly, lines and superficies may be exposed by *section*, namely, a line may be made by cutting an exposed superficies; and a superficies, by the cutting of an exposed solid.

4. *Time* is exposed, not only by the exposition of a line, but also of some moveable thing, which is moved uniformly upon that line, or at least is supposed so to be moved. For, seeing time is an idea of motion, in which we consider former and latter, that is succession, it is not sufficient for the exposition of time that a line be described; but we must also have in our mind an imagination of some moveable thing passing over that line; and the motion of it must be uniform, that time may be divided and compounded as often as there shall be need. And, therefore, when philosophers, in their demonstrations, draw a line, and say, *Let that line be time*, it is to be understood as if they said, *Let the conception of uniform motion upon that line, be time*. For though the circles in dials be lines, yet they are not of themselves sufficient to note time by, except also there be, or be supposed to be, a motion of the shadow or the hand.

5. *Number* is exposed, either by the exposition of points, or of the names of number, *one, two, three, &c.;* and those points must not be contiguous, so as that they cannot be distinguished by notes, but they must be so placed that they may be *discerned* one from another; for, from this it is, that number is called *discreet quantity*, whereas all quantity, which is designed by motion, is called *continual quantity*. But that number may be exposed by the names of number, it is necessary that they be recited by heart and in order, as one, two, three, &c.; for by saying one, one, one, and so forward, we know not what number

we are at beyond two or three; which also appear to us in this manner not as number, but as figure.

6. For the exposition of *velocity,* which, by the definition thereof, is a motion which, in a certain time, passeth over a certain space, it is requisite, not only that time be exposed, but that there be also exposed that space which is transmitted by the body, whose velocity we would determine; and that a body be understood to be moved in that space also; so that there must be exposed two lines, upon one of which uniform motion must be understood to be made, that the time may be determined; and, upon the other,

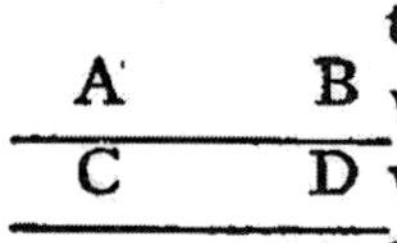

the velocity is to be computed. As if we would expose the velocity of the body A we draw two lines A B and C D, and place a body in C also; which done, we say the velocity of the body A is so great, that it passeth over the line A B in the same time in which the body C passeth over the line C D with uniform motion.

7. *Weight* is exposed by any heavy body, of what matter soever, so it be always alike heavy.

8. The *proportion* of two magnitudes is then exposed, when the magnitudes themselves are exposed, namely, the proportion of equality, when the magnitudes are equal; and of inequality, when they are unequal. For seeing, by the 5th article of the preceding chapter, the proportion of two unequal magnitudes consists in their difference, compared with either of them; and when two unequal magnitudes are exposed, their difference is also exposed; it follows, that when magnitudes, which have proportion to one another, are exposed, their proportion also is exposed with them; and, in like manner, the proportion

of equals, which consists in this, that there is no difference of magnitude betwixt them, is exposed at the same time when the equal magnitudes themselves are exposed. For example, if the exposed lines A B and C D be equal, the proportion of equality is exposed in them; and if the exposed lines, E F and E G be unequal, the proportion which E F has to E G, and that which E G has to E F are also exposed in them; for not only the lines themselves, but also their difference, G F, is exposed. The proportion of unequals is quantity; for the difference, G F, in which it consists, is quantity. But the proportion of equality is not quantity; because, between equals, there is no difference; nor is one equality greater than another, as one inequality is greater than another inequality.

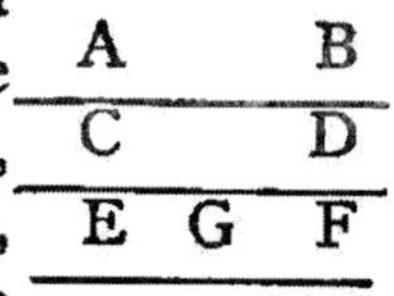

9. The proportion of two *times,* or of two *uniform velocities,* is then exposed, when two lines are exposed by which two bodies are understood to be moved uniformly; and therefore the same two lines serve to exhibit both their own proportion, and that of the times and velocities, according as they are considered to be exposed for the magnitudes themselves, or for the times or velocities. For let the two lines A and B be exposed; their proportion therefore (by the last foregoing article) is exposed; and if they be considered as drawn with equal and uniform velocity, then, seeing their times are greater, or equal, or less, according as the same spaces are transmitted in greater, or equal, or less time, the lines A and B will exhibit the equality or inequality, that is, the proportion of the times. To conclude, if the same lines, A and B, be considered

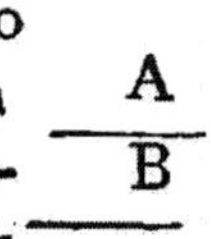

as drawn in the same time, then, seeing their velocities are greater, or equal, or less, according as they pass over in the same time longer or equal, or shorter lines, the same lines, A and B, will exhibit the equality, or inequality, that is, the proportion of their velocities.

CHAPTER XIII.

OF ANALOGISM, OR THE SAME PROPORTION.

1, 2, 3, 4. The nature and definition of proportion, arithmetical and geometrical.—5. The definition, and some properties of the same arithmetical proportion.—6, 7. The definition and transmutations of analogism, or the same geometrical proportion.—8, 9. The definitions of hyperlogism and hypologism, that is, of greater and less proportion, and their transmutations.—10, 11, 12. Comparison of analogical quantities, according to magnitude.—13, 14, 15. Composition of proportions.—16, 17, 18, 19, 20, 21, 22, 23, 24, 25. The definition and properties of continual proportion.—26, 27, 28, 29. Comparison of arithmetical and geometrical proportions.

CHAPTER XIV.

OF STRAIT AND CROOKED, ANGLE AND FIGURE.

1. The definition and properties of a strait line.—2. The definition and properties of a plane superficies.—3. Several sorts of crooked lines.—4. The definition and properties of a circular line.—5. The properties of a strait line taken in a plane.—6. The definition of tangent lines.—7. The definition of an angle, and the kinds thereof.—8. In concentric circles, arches of the same angle are to one another, as the whole circumferences are.—9. The quantity of an angle, in what it consists.—10. The distinction of angles, simply so called.—

11. Of strait lines from the centre of a circle to a tangent of the same.—12. The general definition of parallels, and the properties of strait parallels.—13. The circumferences of circles are to one another, as their diameters are.—14. In triangles, strait lines parallel to the bases are to one another, as the parts of the sides which they cut off from the vertex. —15. By what fraction of a strait line the circumference of a circle is made.—16. That an angle of contingence is quantity, but of a different kind from that of an angle simply so called; and that it can neither add nor take way any thing from the same.—17. That the inclination of planes is angle simply so called.—18. A solid angle, what it is.—19. What is the nature of asymptotes.—20. Situation, by what it is determined.—21. What is like situation; what is figure; and what are like figures.

PART III.

PROPORTIONS OF MOTIONS AND MAGNITUDES.

CHAPTER XV.

OF THE NATURE, PROPERTIES, AND DIVERS CONSIDERATIONS OF MOTION AND ENDEAVOUR.

1. Repetition of some principles of the doctrine of motion formerly set down.—2. Other principles added to them.—3. Certain theorems concerning the nature of motion.—4. Divers considerations of motion.—5. The way by which the first endeavour of bodies moved tendeth.—6. In motion which is made by concourse, one of the movents ceasing, the endeavour is made by the way by which the rest tend.—7. All endeavour is propagated in infinitum.—8. How much greater the velocity or magnitude is of a movent, so much the greater is the efficacy thereof upon any other body in its way.

1. THE next things in order to be treated of are MOTION and MAGNITUDE, which are the most common accidents of all bodies. This place therefore most properly belongs to the elements of geometry. But because this part of philosophy, having been improved by the best wits of all ages, has afforded greater plenty of matter than can well be thrust together within the narrow limits of this discourse, I thought fit to admonish the reader, that before he proceeded further, he take

into his hands the works of Euclid, Archimedes, Apollonius, and other as well ancient as modern writers. For to what end is it, to do over again that which is already done? The little therefore that I shall say concerning geometry in some of the following chapters, shall be such only as is new, and conducing to natural philosophy.

I have already delivered some of the principles of this doctrine in the eighth and ninth chapters; which I shall briefly put together here, that the reader in going on may have their light nearer at hand.

First, therefore, in chap. viii, art. 10, *motion* is defined to be *the continual privation of one place, and acquisition of another.*

Secondly, it is there shown, that *whatsoever is moved is moved in time.*

Thirdly, in the same chapter, art. 11, I have defined *rest to be when a body remains for some time in one place.*

Fourthly, it is there shown, that *whatsoever is moved is not in any determined place;* as also that the same *has been moved, is still moved, and will yet be moved;* so that in every part of that space, in which motion is made, we may consider three times, namely, the *past,* the *present,* and the *future time.*

Fifthly, in art. 15 of the same chapter, I have defined *velocity* or *swiftness to be motion considered as power, namely, that power by which a body moved may in a certain time transmit a certain length;* which also may more briefly be enunciated thus, *velocity is the quantity of motion determined by time and line.*

Sixthly, in the same chapter, art. 16, I have shown that *motion is the measure of time.*

Seventhly, in the same chapter, art. 17, I have defined

motions to be equally swift, when in equal times equal lengths are transmitted by them.

Eighthly, in art. 18 of the same chapter, *motions* are defined to be *equal, when the swiftness of one moved body, computed in every part of its magnitude, is equal to the swiftness of another, computed also in every part of its magnitude.* From whence it is to be noted, that *motions equal to one another, and motions equally swift,* do not signify the same thing; for when two horses draw abreast, the motion of both is greater than the motion of either of them singly; but the swiftness of both together is but equal to that of either.

Ninthly, in art. 19 of the same chapter, I have shown, that *whatsoever is at rest will always be at rest, unless there be some other body besides it, which by getting into its place suffers it no longer to remain at rest.* And that *whatsoever is moved, will always be moved, unless there be some other body besides it, which hinders its motion.*

Tenthly, in chap. IX, art. 7, I have demonstrated that *when any body is moved which was formerly at rest, the immediate efficient cause of that motion is in some other moved and contiguous body.*

Eleventhly, I have shown in the same place, that *whatsoever is moved, will always be moved in the same way, and with the same swiftness, if it be not hindered by some other moved and contiguous body.*

2. To which principles I shall here add those that follow. First, I define ENDEAVOUR *to be motion made in less space and time than can be given;* that is *less than can be determined or assigned by exposition or number;* that is, *motion made through the length of a point, and in an instant or point of time.* For the explaining of which definition it must be remembered,

that by a point is not to be understood that which has no quantity, or which cannot by any means be divided; for there is no such thing in nature; but that, whose quantity is not at all considered, that is, whereof neither quantity nor any part is computed in demonstration; so that a point is not to be taken for an indivisible, but for an undivided thing; as also an instant is to be taken for an undivided, and not for an indivisible time.

In like manner, endeavour is to be conceived as motion; but so as that neither the quantity of the time in which, nor of the line in which it is made, may in demonstration be at all brought into comparison with the quantity of that time, or of that line of which it is a part. And yet, as a point may be compared with a point, so one endeavour may be compared with another endeavour, and one may be found to be greater or less than another. For if the vertical points of two angles be compared, they will be equal or unequal in the same proportion which the angles themselves have to one another. Or if a strait line cut many circumferences of concentric circles, the inequality of the points of intersection will be in the same proportion which the perimeters have to one another. And in the same manner, if two motions begin and end both together, their endeavours will be equal or unequal, according to the proportion of their velocities; as we see a bullet of lead descend with greater endeavour than a ball of wool.

Secondly, I define IMPETUS, *or quickness of motion, to be the swiftness or velocity of the body moved, but considered in the several points of that time in which it is moved. In which sense* impetus *is nothing else but the quantity or velocity of endeavour. But considered with the whole time, it is the whole velocity of the body moved taken together throughout all the time, and equal to the product of a line representing the time, multiplied into a line representing the arithmetically mean* impetus *or quickness.* Which arithmetical mean, what it is, is defined in the 29th article of chapter XIII.

And because in equal times the ways that are passed are as the velocities, and the *impetus* is the velocity they go withal, reckoned in all the several points of the times, it followeth that during any time whatsoever, howsoever the *impetus* be increased or decreased, the length of the way passed over shall be increased or decreased in the same proportion; and the same line shall represent both the way of the body moved, and the several *impetus* or degrees of swiftness wherewith the way is passed over.

And if the body moved be not a point, but a strait line moved so as that every point thereof make a several strait line, the plane described by its motion, whether uniform, accelerated, or retarded, shall be greater or less, the time being the same, in the same proportion with that of the *impetus* reckoned in one motion to the *impetus* reckoned in the other. For the reason is the same in parallelograms and their sides.

* * * * * * * * *

Thirdly, I define RESISTANCE *to be the endeavour of one moved body either wholly or in part contrary to the endeavour of another moved body, which toucheth the same.* I say, wholly contrary, when the endeavour of two bodies proceeds in the same strait line from the opposite extremes, and contrary in part, when two bodies have their endeavour in two lines, which, proceeding from the extreme points of a strait line, meet without the same.

Fourthly, that I may define what it is to PRESS, I say,

that *of two moved bodies one presses the other, when with its endeavour it makes either all or part of the other body to go out of its place.*

Fifthly, *a body which is pressed and not wholly removed, is said to* RESTORE *itself, when, the pressing body being taken away, the parts which were moved do, by reason of the internal constitution of the pressed body, return every one into its own place.* And this we may observe in springs, in blown bladders, and in many other bodies, whose parts yield more or less to the endeavour which the pressing body makes at the first arrival; but afterwards, when the pressing body is removed, they do, by some force within them, *restore* themselves, and give their whole body the same figure it had before.

Sixthly, I define FORCE *to be the* impetus *or quickness of motion multiplied either into itself, or into the magnitude of the movent, by means whereof the said movent works more or less upon the body that resists it.*

3. Having premised thus much, I shall now demonstrate, first, that if a point moved come to touch another point which is at rest, how little soever the impetus or quickness of its motion be, it shall move that other point. For if by that impetus it do not at all move it out of its place, neither shall it move it with double the same impetus. For nothing doubled is still nothing; and for the same reason it shall never move it with that impetus, how many times soever it be multiplied, because nothing, however it be multiplied, will for ever be nothing. Wherefore, when a point is at rest, if it do not yield to the least impetus, it will yield to none; and consequently it will be impossible that that, which is at rest, should ever be moved.

Secondly, that when a point moved, how little soever the impetus thereof be, falls upon a point of any body at rest, how hard soever that body be, it will at the first touch make it yield a little. For if it do not yield to the impetus which is in that point, neither will it yield to the impetus of never so many points, which have all their impetus severally equal to the impetus of that point. For seeing all those points together work equally, if any one of them have no effect, the aggregate of them all together shall have no effect as many times told as there are points in the whole body, that is, still no effect at all; and by consequent there would be some bodies so hard that it would be impossible to break them; that is, a finite hardness, or a finite force, would not yield to that which is infinite; which is absurd.

Coroll. It is therefore manifest, that rest does nothing at all, nor is of any efficacy; and that nothing but motion gives motion to such things as be at rest, and takes it from things moved.

Thirdly, that cessation in the movent does not cause cessation in that which was moved by it. For (by number 11 of art. 1 of this chapter) whatsoever is moved perseveres in the same way and with the same swiftness, as long as it is not hindered by something that is moved against it. Now it is manifest, that cessation is not contrary motion; and therefore it follows that the standing still of the movent does not make it necessary that the thing moved should also stand still.

Coroll. They are therefore deceived, that reckon the taking away of the impediment or resistance for one of the causes of motion.

4. Motion is brought into account for divers respects; first, as in a body *undivided*, that is, considered

as a point; or, as in a *divided* body. In an undivided body, when we suppose the way, by which the motion is made, to be a line; and in a divided body, when we compute the motion of the several parts of that body, as of parts.

Secondly, from the diversity of the regulation of motion, it is in body, considered as undivided, sometimes *uniform* and sometimes *multiform*. *Uniform* is that by which equal lines are always transmitted in equal times; and *multiform*, when in one time more, in another time less space is transmitted. Again, of multiform motions, there are some in which the degrees of acceleration and retardation proceed in the same proportions, which the spaces transmitted have, whether duplicate, or triplicate, or by whatsoever number multiplied; and others in which it is otherwise.

Thirdly, from the number of the movents; that is, one motion is made by one movent only, and another by the concourse of many movents.

Fourthly, from the position of that line in which a body is moved, in respect of some other line; and from hence one motion is called *perpendicular*, another *oblique*, another *parallel*.

Fifthly, from the position of the movent in respect of the moved body; from whence one motion is *pulsion* or driving, another *traction* or drawing. *Pulsion*, when the movent makes the moved body go before it; and *traction*, when it makes it follow. Again there are two sorts of *pulsion*; one, when the motions of the movent and moved body begin both together, which may be called the *trusion* or *thrusting* and *vection*; the other, when the movent is first moved, and afterwards the moved body, which motion is called *percussion* or *stroke*.

Sixthly, motion is considered sometimes from the effect only which the movent works in the moved body, which is usually called *moment.* Now *moment is the excess of motion which the movent has above the motion or endeavour of the resisting body.*

Seventhly, it may be considered from the diversity of the *medium;* as one motion may be made in *vacuity* or *empty place;* another in a *fluid;* another in a *consistent medium,* that is, a *medium* whose parts are by some power so *consistent* and *cohering,* that no part of the same will yield to the movent, unless the whole yield also.

Eighthly, when a moved body is considered as having parts, there arises another distinction of motion into *simple* and *compound. Simple,* when all the several parts describe several equal lines; *compounded,* when the lines described are unequal.

5. All endeavour tends towards that part, that is to say, in that way which is determined by the motion of the movent, if the movent be but one; or, if there be many movents, in that way which their concourse determines. For example, if a moved body have direct motion, its first endeavour will be in a strait line; if it have circular motion, its first endeavour will be in the circumference of a circle.

6. And whatsoever the line be, in which a body has its motion from the concourse of two movents, as soon as in any point thereof the force of one of the movents ceases, there immediately the former endeavour of that body will be changed into an endeavour in the line of the other movent.

Wherefore, when any body is carried on by the concourse of two winds, one of those winds ceasing, the endeavour and motion of that body will be in that line, in which it would have been carried by that wind alone which blows still. And in the describing of a circle, where that which is moved has its motion determined by a movent in a tangent, and by the radius which keeps it in a certain distance from the centre, if the retention of the radius cease, that endeavour, which was in the circumference of the circle, will now be in the tangent, that is, in a strait line. For, seeing endeavour is computed in a less part of the circumference than can be given, that is, in a point, the way by which a body is moved in the circumference is compounded of innumerable strait lines, of which every one is less than can be given; which are therefore called points. Wherefore when any body, which is moved in the circumference of a circle, is freed from the retention of the radius, it will proceed in one of those strait lines, that is, in a tangent.

7. All endeavour, whether strong or weak, is propagated to infinite distance; for it is motion. If therefore the first endeavour of a body be made in space which is empty, it will always proceed with the same velocity; for it cannot be supposed that it can receive any resistance at all from empty space; and therefore, (by art. 7, chap. IX) will always proceed in the same way and with the same swiftness. And if its endeavour be in space which is filled, yet, seeing endeavour is motion, that which stands next in its way shall be removed, and endeavour further, and again remove that which stands next, and so infinitely. Wherefore the propagation of endeavour, from one part of full space to another, proceeds infinitely. Besides, it reaches in any instant to any distance, how great soever. For in the same instant in which the first part of the full *medium* removes that which is next it, the second also removes

that part which is next to it; and therefore all endeavour, whether it be in empty or in full space, proceeds not only to any distance, how great soever, but also in any time, how little soever, that is, in an instant. Nor makes it any matter, that endeavour, by proceeding, grows weaker and weaker, till at last it can no longer be perceived by sense; for motion may be insensible; and I do not here examine things by sense and experience, but by reason.

8. When two movents are of equal magnitude, the swifter of them works with greater force than the slower, upon a body that resists their motion. Also, if two movents have equal velocity, the greater of them works with more force than the less. For where the magnitude is equal, the movent of greater velocity makes the greater impression upon that body upon which it falls; and where the velocity is equal, the movent of greater magnitude falling upon the same point, or an equal part of another body, loses less of its velocity, because the resisting body works only upon that part of the movent which it touches, and therefore abates the impetus of that part only; whereas in the mean time the parts, which are not touched, proceed, and retain their whole force, till they also come to be touched; and their force has some effect. Wherefore, for example, in batteries a longer than a shorter piece of timber of the same thickness and velocitcy, and a thicker than a slenderer piece of the same length and velocity, work a greater effect upon the wall.

CHAPTER XVI.

OF MOTION ACCELERATED AND UNIFORM, AND OF MOTION BY CONCOURSE.

1. The velocity of any body, in what time soever it be computed, is that which is made of the multiplication of the impetus, or quickness of its motion into the time.—2-5. In all motion, the lengths which are passed through are to one another, as the products made by the impetus multiplied into the time.—6. If two bodies be moved with uniform motion through two lengths, the proportion of those lengths to one another will be compounded of the proportions of time to time, and impetus to impetus, directly taken.—7. If two bodies pass through two lengths with uniform motion, the proportion of their time to one another will be compounded of the proportions of length to length, and impetus to impetus reciprocally taken; also the proportion of their impetus to one another will be compounded of the proportions of length to length, and time to time reciprocally taken.—8. If a body be carried on with uniform motion by two movents together, which meet in an angle, the line by which it passes will be a strait line, subtending the complement of that angle to two right angles.—9, &c. If a body be carried by two movents together, one of them being moved with uniform, the other with accelerated motion, and the proportion of their lengths to their times being explicable in numbers, how to find out what line that body describes.

CHAPTER XVII.

OF FIGURES DEFICIENT.

1. Definitions of a deficient figure; of a complete figure; of the complement of a deficient figure; and of proportions which are proportional and commensurable to one another.—2. The proportion of a deficient figure to its complement.—3. The proportions of deficient figures to the parallelograms in

which they are described, set forth in a table.—4. The description and production of the same figures.—5. The drawing of tangents to them.—6. In what proportion the same figures exceed a strait-lined triangle of the same altitude and base.—7. A table of solid deficient figures described in a cylinder.—8. In what proportion the same figures exceed a cone of the same altitude and base.—9. How a plain deficient figure may be described in a parallelogram, so that it be to a triangle of the same base and altitude, as another deficient figure, plain or solid, twice taken, is to the same deficient figure, together with the complete figure in which it is described.—10. The transferring of certain properties of deficient figures described in a parallelogram to the proportions of the spaces transmitted with several degrees of velocity.—11. Of deficient figures described in a circle.—12. The proposition demonstrated in art. 2 confirmed from the elements of philosophy.—13. An unusual way of reasoning concerning the equality between the superficies of a portion of a sphere and a circle.—14. How from the description of deficient figures in a parallelogram, any number of mean proportionals may be found out between two given strait lines.

CHAPTER XVIII.

OF THE EQUATION OF STRAIT LINES WITH THE CROOKED LINES OF PARABOLAS AND OTHER FIGURES MADE IN IMITATION OF PARABOLAS.

1. To find the strait line equal to the crooked line of a semiparabola.—2. To find a strait line equal to the crooked line of the first semiparabolaster, or to the crooked line of any other of the deficient figures of the table of the 3d article of the precedent chapter.

CHAPTER XIX.

OF ANGLES OF INCIDENCE AND REFLECTION, EQUAL BY SUPPOSITION.

1. If two strait lines falling upon another strait line be parallel, the lines reflected from them shall also be parallel.—2. If two strait lines drawn from one point fall upon another strait line, the lines reflected from them, if they be drawn out the other way, will meet in an angle equal to the angle made by the lines of incidence.—3. If two strait parallel lines, drawn not oppositely, but from the same parts, fall upon the circumference of a circle, the lines reflected from them, if produced they meet within the circle, will make an angle double to that which is made by two strait lines drawn from the centre to the points of incidence.—4. If two strait lines drawn from the same point without a circle fall upon the circumference, and the lines reflected from them being produced meet within the circle, they will make an angle equal to twice that angle, which is made by two strait lines drawn from the centre to the points of incidence, together with the angle which the incident lines themselves make.—5. If two strait lines drawn from one point fall upon the concave circumference of a circle, and the angle they make be less than twice the angle at the centre, the lines reflected from them and meeting within the circle will make an angle, which being added to the angle of the incident lines will be equal to twice the angle at the centre.—6. If through any one point two unequal chords be drawn cutting one another, and the centre of the circle be not placed between them, and the lines reflected from them concur wheresoever, there cannot through the point, through which the two former lines were drawn, be drawn any other strait line whose reflected line shall pass through the common point of the two former lines reflected.—7. In equal chords the same is not true.—8. Two points being given in the circumference of a circle, to draw two strait lines to them, so that their reflected lines may contain any angle given.—9. If a strait line falling upon the circumference of a circle be produced till it reach the

semidiameter, and that part of it, which is intercepted between the circumference and the semidiameter, be equal to that part of the semidiameter which is between the point of concourse and the centre, the reflected line will be parallel to the semidiameter.—10. If from a point within a circle, two strait lines be drawn to the circumference, and their reflected lines meet in the circumference of the same circle, the angle made by the reflected lines will be a third part of the angle made by the incident lines.

CHAPTER XX.

OF THE DIMENSION OF A CIRCLE, AND THE DIVISION OF ANGLES OR ARCHES.

1. The dimension of a circle never determined in numbers by Archimedes and others.—2. The first attempt for the finding out of the dimension of a circle by lines.—3. The second attempt for the finding out of the dimension of a circle from the consideration of the nature of crookedness.—4. The third attempt; and some things propounded to be further searched into.—5. The equation of the spiral of Archimedes with a strait line.—6. Of the analysis of geometricians by the powers of lines.

CHAPTER XXI.

OF CIRCULAR MOTION.

1. In simple motion, every strait line taken in the body moved is so carried, that it is always parallel to the places in which it formerly was.—2. If circular motion be made about a resting centre, and in that circle there be an epicycle, whose revolution is made the contrary way, in such manner that in equal times it make equal angles, every strait line taken in that epicycle will be so carried, that it will always be parallel to the places in which it formerly was.—3. The properties of simple motion.—4. If a fluid be moved with simple

circular motion, all the points taken in it will describe their circles in times proportional to the distances from the centre.—5. Simple motion dissipates heterogeneous and congregates homogeneous bodies.—6. If a circle made by a movent moved with simple motion be commensurable to another circle made by a point which is carried about by the same movent, all the points of both the circles will at some time return to the same situation.—7. If a sphere have simple motion, its motion will more dissipate heterogeneous bodies by how much it is more remote from the poles.—8. If the simple circular motion of a fluid body be hindered by a body which is not fluid, the fluid body will spread itself upon the superficies of that body.—9. Circular motion about a fixed centre casteth off by the tangent such things as lie upon the circumference and stick not to it.—10. Such things, as are moved with simple circular motion, beget simple circular motion.—11. If that which is so moved have one side hard and the other side fluid, its motion will not be perfectly circular.

CHAPTER XXII.

OF OTHER VARIETY OF MOTION.

1. Endeavour and pressure how they differ.—2. Two kinds of mediums in which bodies are moved.—3. Propagation of motion, what it is.—4. What motion bodies have, when they press one another.—5. Fluid bodies, when they are pressed together, penetrate one another.—6. When one body presseth another and doth not penetrate it, the action of the pressing body is perpendicular to the superficies of the body pressed.—7. When a hard body, pressing another body, penetrates the same, it doth not penetrate it perpendicularly, unless it fall perpendicularly upon it.—8. Motion sometimes opposite to that of the movent.—9. In a full medium, motion is propagated to any distance.—10. Dilatation and contraction what they are.—11. Dilatation and contraction suppose mutation of the smallest parts in respect of their situation.—12. All traction is pulsion.—13. Such things as being pressed or bent restore themselves, have motion in their internal parts.—

14. Though that which carrieth another be stopped, the body carried will proceed.—15, 16. The effects of percussion not to be compared with those of weight.—17, 18: Motion cannot begin first in the internal parts of the body.—19. Action and reaction proceed in the same line.—20. Habit, what it is.

CHAPTER XXIII.

OF THE CENTRE OF EQUIPONDERATION; OF BODIES PRESSING DOWNWARDS IN STRAIT PARALLEL LINES.

1. Definitions and suppositions.—2. Two planes of equiponderation are not parallel.—3. The centre of equiponderation is in every plane of equiponderation.—4. The moments of equal ponderants are to one another as their distances from the centre of the scale.—5, 6.. The moments of unequal ponderants have their proportion to one another compounded of the proportions of their weights and distances from the centre of the scale.—7. If two ponderants have their weights and distances from the centre of the scale in reciprocal proportion, they are equally poised; and contrarily.—8. If the parts of any ponderant press the beams of the scale everywhere equally, all the parts cut off, reckoned from the centre of the scale, will have their moments in the same proportion with that of the parts of a triangle cut off from the vertex by strait lines parallel to the base.—9. The diameter of equiponderation of figures, which are deficient according to commensurable proportions of their altitudes and bases, divides the axis, so that the part taken next the vertex is to the other part of the complete figure to the deficient figure.—10. The diameter of equiponderation of the complement of the half of any of the said deficient figures, divides that line which is drawn through the vertex parallel to the base, so that the part next the vertex is to the other part of the complete figure to the complement.—11. The centre of equiponderation of the half of any of the deficient figures in the first row of the table of art. 3, chap. xvii, may be found out by the numbers of the second row.—12. The centre of equiponderation of the half of any of the figures of the second

row of the same table, may be found out by the numbers of the fourth row.—13. The centre of equiponderation of the half of any of the figures in the same table being known, the centre of the excess of the same figure above a triangle of the same altitude and base is also known.—14. The centre of equiponderation of a solid sector is in the axis so divided, that the part next the vertex be to the whole axis, wanting half the axis of the portion of the sphere, as 3 to 4.

CHAPTER XXIV.

OF REFRACTION AND REFLECTION.

1. Definitions.—2. In perpendicular motion there is no refraction.—3. Things thrown out of a thinner into a thicker medium are so refracted that the angle refracted is greater than the angle of inclination.—4. Endeavour, which from one point tendeth every way, will be so refracted, as that the sine of the angle refracted will be to the sine of the angle of inclination, as the density of the first medium is to the density of the second medium, reciprocally taken.—5. The sine of the refracted angle in one inclination is to the sine of the refracted angle in another inclination, as the sine of the angle of that inclination is to the sine of the angle of this inclination.—6. If two lines of incidence, having equal inclination, be the one in a thinner, the other in a thicker medium, the sine of the angle of inclination will be a mean proportional between the two sines of the refracted angles.—7. If the angle of inclination be semirect, and the line of inclination be in the thicker medium, and the proportion of their densities be the same with that of the diagonal to the side of a square, and the separating superficies be plane, the refracted line will be in the separating superficies.—8. If a body be carried in a strait line upon another body, and do not penetrate the same, but be reflected from it, the angle of reflection will be equal to the angle of incidence.—9. The same happens in the generation of motion in the line of incidence.

PART IV.

PHYSICS, OR THE PHENOMENA OF NATURE.

CHAPTER XXV.*

OF SENSE AND ANIMAL MOTION.

1. The connexion of what hath been said with that which followeth.—2. The investigation of the nature of sense, and the definition of sense.—3. The subject and object of sense.—4. The organs of sense.—5. All bodies are not indued with sense.—6. But one phantasm at one and the same time.—7. Imagination the remains of past sense, which also is memory. Of sleep.—8. How phantasms succeed one another.—9. Dreams, whence they proceed.—10. Of the senses, their kinds, their organs, and phantasms proper and common.—11. The magnitude of images, how and by what it is determined.—12. Pleasure, pain, appetite and aversion, what they are.—13. Deliberation and will, what.

1. I HAVE, in the first chapter, defined philosophy to be *knowledge of effects acquired by true ratiocination, from knowledge first had of their causes and generation; and of such causes or generations as may be, from former knowledge of their effects or appearances.* There are, therefore, two methods of philosophy; one, from the generation of things to their possible effects; and the other, from their effects or ap-

* For list of the writings of Hobbes on psychology, cf. p. xx.

pearances to some possible generation of the same. In the former of these the truth of the first principles of our ratiocination, namely definitions, is made and constituted by ourselves, whilst we consent and agree about the appellations of things. And this part I have finished in the foregoing chapters; in which, if I am not deceived, I have affirmed nothing, saving the definitions themselves, which hath not good coherence with the definitions I have given; that is to say, which is not sufficiently demonstrated to all those, that agree with me in the use of words and appellations; for whose sake only I have written the same. I now enter upon the other part; which is the finding out by the appearances or effects of nature, which we know by sense, some ways and means by which they may be, I do not say they are, generated. The principles, therefore, upon which the following discourse depends, are not such as we ourselves make and pronounce in general terms, as definitions; but such, as being placed in the things themselves by the Author of Nature, are by us observed in them; and we make use of them in single and particular, not universal propositions. Nor do they impose upon us any necessity of constituting theorems; their use being only, though not without such general propositions as have been already demonstrated, to show us the possibility of some production or generation. Seeing, therefore, the science, which is here taught, hath its principles in the appearances of nature, and endeth in the attaining of some knowledge of natural causes, I have given to this part the title of PHYSICS, or the *Phenomena of Nature.* Now such things as appear, or are shown to us by nature, we call phenomena or appearances.

Of all the phenomena or appearances which are

near us, the most admirable is apparition itself, τό φαίνεσθαι; namely, that some natural bodies have in themselves the patterns almost of all things, and others of none at all. So that if the appearances be the principles by which we know all other things, we must needs acknowledge sense to be the principle by which we know those principles, and that all the knowledge we have is derived from it. And as for the causes of sense, we cannot begin our search of them from any other phenomenon than that of sense itself. But you will say, by what sense shall we take notice of sense? I answer, by sense itself, namely, by the memory which for some time remains in us of things sensible, though they themselves pass away. For he that perceives that he hath perceived, remembers.

In the first place, therefore, the causes of our perception, that is, the causes of those ideas and phantasms which are perpetually generated within us whilst we make use of our senses, are to be enquired into; and in what manner their generation proceeds. To help which inquisition, we may observe first of all, that our phantasms or ideas are not always the same; but that new ones appear to us, and old ones vanish, according as we apply our organs of sense, now to one object, now to another. Wherefore they are generated, and perish. And from hence it is manifest, that they are some change or mutation in the sentient.

2. Now that all mutation or alteration is motion or endeavour (and endeavour also is motion) in the internal parts of the thing that is altered, hath been proved (in art. 9, chap. VIII) from this, that whilst even the least parts of any body remain in the same situation in respect of one another, it cannot be said that any alteration, unless perhaps that the whole body

together hath been moved, hath happened to it; but that it both appeareth and is the same it appeared and was before. Sense, therefore, in the sentient, can be nothing else but motion in some of the internal parts of the sentient; and the parts so moved are parts of the organs of sense. For the parts of our body, by which we perceive any thing, are those we commonly call the organs of sense. And so we find what is the subject of our sense, namely, that in which are the phantasms; and partly also we have discovered the nature of sense, namely, that it is some internal motion in the sentient.

I have shown besides (in chap. IX, art. 7) that no motion is generated but by a body contiguous and moved: from whence it is manifest, that the immediate cause of sense or perception consists in this, that the first organ of sense is touched and pressed. For when the uttermost part of the organ is pressed, it no sooner yields, but the part next within it is pressed also; and, in this manner, the pressure or motion is propagated through all the parts of the organ to the innermost. And thus also the pressure of the uttermost part proceeds from the pressure of some more remote body, and so continually, till we come to that from which, as from its fountain, we derive the phantasm or idea that is made in us by our sense. And this, whatsoever it be, is that we commonly call *the object.* Sense, therefore, is some internal motion in the sentient, generated by some internal motion of the parts of the object, and propagated through all the media to the innermost part of the organ. By which words I have almost defined what sense is.

Moreover, I have shown (art. 2, chap. XV) that all resistance is endeavour opposite to another endeavour, that is to say, reaction. Seeing, therefore, there is in the whole organ, by reason of it own internal natural motion, some resistance or reaction against the motion which is propagated from the object to the innermost part of the organ, there is also in the same organ an endeavour opposite to the endeavour which proceeds from the object; so that when that endeavour inwards is the last action in the act of sense, then from the reaction, how little soever the duration of it be, a phantasm or idea hath its being; which, by reason that the endeavour is now outwards, doth always appear as something situate without the organ. So that now I shall give you the whole definition of sense, as it is drawn from the explication of the causes thereof and the order of its generation, thus: SENSE *is a phantasm, made by the reaction and endeavour outwards in the organ of sense, caused by an endeavour inwards from the object, remaining for some time more or less.*

3. The *subject* of sense is the *sentient* itself, namely, some living creature; and we speak more correctly, when we say a living creature seeth, than when we say the eye seeth. The object is the thing received; and it is more accurately said, that we see the sun, than that we see the light. For light and colour, and heat and sound, and other qualities which are commonly called sensible, are not objects, but phantasms in the sentients. For a phantasm is the act of sense, and differs no otherwise from sense than *fieri,* that is, being a doing, differs from *factum esse,* that is, being done; which difference, in things that are done in an instant, is none at all; and a phantasm is made in an instant. For in all motion which proceeds by perpetual propagation, the first part being moved moves the second, the second the third, and so on to the last, and that to any distance, how great soever. And in what

point of time the first or foremost part proceeded to the place of the second, which is thrust on, in the same point of time the last save one proceeded into the place of the last yielding part; which by reaction, in the same instant, if the reaction be strong enough, makes a phantasm; and a phantasm being made, perception is made together with it.

4. The *organs* of sense, which are in the sentient, are such parts thereof, that if they be hurt, the very generation of phantasms is thereby destroyed, though all the rest of the parts remain entire. Now these parts in the most of living creatures are found to be certain spirits and membranes, which, proceeding from the *pia mater,* involve the brain and all the nerves; also the brain itself, and the arteries which are in the brain; and such other parts, as being stirred, the heart also, which is the fountain of all sense, is stirred together with them. For whensoever the action of the object reacheth the body of the sentient, that action is by some nerve propagated to the brain; and if the nerve leading thither be so hurt or obstructed, that the motion can be propagated no further, no sense follows. Also if the motion be intercepted between the brain and the heart by the defect of the organ by which the action is proagated, there will be no perception of the object.

5. But though all sense, as I have said, be made by reaction, nevertheless it is not necessary that every thing that reacteth should have sense. I know there have been philosophers, and those learned men, who have maintained that all bodies are endued with sense. Nor do I see how they can be refuted, if the nature of sense be placed in reaction only. And, though by the reaction of bodies inanimate a phantasm might be made, it would nevertheless cease, as soon as ever the object

were removed. For unless those bodies had organs, as living creatures have, fit for the retaining of such motion as is made in them, their sense would be such, as that they should never remember the same. And therefore this hath nothing to do with that sense which is the subject of my discourse. For by sense, we commonly understand the judgment we make of objects by their phantasms; namely, by comparing and distinguishing those phantasms; which we could never do, if that motion in the organ, by which the phantasm is made, did not remain there for some time, and make the same phantasm return. Wherefore sense, as I here understand it, and which is commonly so called, hath necessarily some memory adhering to it, by which former and later phantasms may be compared together, and distinguished from one another.

Sense, therefore, properly so called, must necessarily have in it a perpetual variety of phantasms, that they may be discerned one from another. For if we should suppose a man to be made with clear eyes, and all the rest of his organs of sight well disposed, but endued with no other sense; and that he should look only upon one thing, which is always of the same colour and figure, without the least appearance of variety, he would seem to me, whatsoever others may say, to see, no more than I seem to myself to feel the bones of my own limbs by my organs of feeling; and yet those bones are always and on all sides touched by a most sensible membrane. I might perhaps say he were astonished, and looked upon it; but I should not say he saw it; it being almost all one for a man to be always sensible of one and the same thing, and not to be sensible at all of any thing.

6. And yet such is the nature of sense, that it does

not permit a man to discern many things at once. For seeing the nature of sense consists in motion; as long as the organs are employed about one object, they cannot be so moved by another at the same time, as to make by both their motions one sincere phantasm of each of them at once. And therefore two several phantasms will not be made by two objects working together, but only one phantasm compounded from the action of both.

Besides, as when we divide a body, we divide its place; and when we reckon many bodies, we must necessarily reckon as many places; and contrarily, as I have shown in the seventh chapter; so what number soever we say there be at times, we must understand the same number of motions also; and as oft as we count many motions, so oft we reckon many times. For though the object we look upon be of divers colours, yet with those divers colours it is but one varied object, and not variety of objects.

Moreover, whilst those organs which are common to all the senses, such as are those parts of every organ which proceed in men from the root of the nerves to the heart, are vehemently stirred by a strong action from some one object, they are, by reason of the contumacy which the motion, they have already, gives them against the reception of all other motion, made the less fit to receive any other impression from whatsoever other objects, to what sense soever those objects belong. And hence it is, that an earnest studying of one object, takes away the sense of all other objects for the present. For *study* is nothing else but a possession of the mind, that is to say, a vehement motion made by some one object in the organs of sense, which are stupid to all other motions as long as this lasteth; according to what was said by Terence, " *Populus studio stupidus in funambulo animum occuparat.*" For what is *stupor* but that which the Greeks called ἀναισθησία, that, is, a cessation from the sense of other things? Wherefore at one and the same time, we cannot by sense perceive more than one single object; as in reading, we see the letters successively one by one, and not all together, though the whole page be presented to our eye; and though every several letter be distinctly written there, yet when we look upon the whole page at once, we read nothing.

From hence it is manifest, that every endeavour of the organ outwards, is not to be called sense, but that only, which at several times is by vehemence made stronger and more predominate than the rest; which deprives us of the sense of other phantasms, no otherwise than the sun deprives the rest of the stars of light not by hindering their action, but by obscuring and hiding them with his excess of brightness.

7. But the motion of the organ, by which a phantasm is made, is not commonly called sense, except the object be present. And the phantasm remaining after the object is removed or past by, is called *fancy*, and in Latin *imaginatio;* which word, because all phantasms are not images, doth not fully answer the signification of the word *fancy* in its general acceptation. Nevertheless I may use it safely enough, by understanding it for the Greek Φαντασία.

IMAGINATION therefore is nothing else but *sense decaying*, or *weakened*, by the absence of the object. But what may be the cause of this decay or weakening? Is the motion the weaker, because the object is taken away? If it were, then phantasms would always and necessarily be less clear in the imagination, than they are in sense; which is not true. For in dreams, which are the imaginations of those that sleep, they are no less clear than in sense itself. But the reason why in men waking the phantasms of things past are more obscure than those of things present, is this, that their organs being at the same time moved by other present objects, those phantasms are the less predominate. Whereas in sleep, the passages being shut up, external action doth not at all disturb or hinder internal motion.

If this be true, the next thing to be considered, will be, whether any cause may be found out, from the supposition whereof it will follow, that the passage is shut up from the external objects of sense to the internal organ. I suppose, therefore, that by the continual action of objects, to which a reaction of the organ, and more especially of the spirits, is necessarily consequent, the organ is wearied, that is, its parts are no longer moved by the spirits without some pain; and consequently the nerves being abandoned and grown slack, they retire to their fountain, which is the cavity either of the brain or of the heart; by which means the action which proceeded by the nerves is necessarily intercepted. For action upon a patient, that retires from it, makes but little impression at the first; and at last, when the nerves are by little and little slackened, none at all. And therefore there is no more reaction, that is, no more sense, till the organ being refreshed by rest, and by a supply of new spirits recovering strength and motion, the sentient awaketh. And thus it seems to be always, unless some other preternatural cause intervene; as heat in the internal parts from lassitude, or from some disease stirring the spirits and other parts of the organ in some extraordinary manner.

8. Now it is not without cause, nor so casual a

thing as many perhaps think it, that phantasms in this their great variety proceed from one another; and that the same phantasms sometimes bring into the mind other phantasms like themselves, and at other times extremely unlike. For in the motion of any continued body, one part follows another by cohesion; and therefore, whilst we turn our eyes and other organs successively to many objects, the motion which was made by every one of them remaining, the phantasms are renewed as often as any one of those motions comes to be predominant above the rest; and they become predominant in the same order in which at any time formerly they were generated by sense. So that when by length of time very many phantasms have been generated within us by sense, then almost any thought may arise from any other thought; insomuch that it may seem to be a thing indifferent and casual, which thought shall follow which. But for the most part this is not so uncertain a thing to waking as to sleeping men. For the thought or phantasm of the desired end brings in all the phantasms, that are means conducing to that end, and that in order backwards from the last to the first, and again forwards from the beginning to the end. But this supposes both appetite, and judgment to discern what means conduce to the end, which is gotten by experience; and experience is store of phantasms, arising from the sense of very many things. For φαντάζεσθαι and *meminisse, fancy* and *memory,* differ only in this, that memory supposeth the time past, which fancy doth not. In memory, the phantasms we consider are as if they were worn out with time; but in our fancy we consider them as they are; which distinction is not of the things themselves, but of the considerations of the sentient. For there is in memory something like that which happens in looking upon things at a great distance; in which as the small parts of the object are not discerned, by reason of their remoteness; so in memory, many accidents and places and parts of things, which were formerly perceived by sense, are by length of time decayed and lost.

The perpetual arising of phantasms, both in sense and imagination, is that which we commonly call discourse of the mind, and is common to men with other living creatures. For he that thinketh, compareth the phantasms that pass, that is, taketh notice of their likeness or unlikeness, to one another. And as he that observes readily the likenesses of things of different natures, or that are very remote from one another, is said to have a good fancy; so he is said to have a good judgment, that finds out the unlikenesses or differences of things that are like one another. Now this observation of differences is not perception made by a common organ of sense, distinct from sense or perception properly so called, but is memory of the differences of particular phantasms remaining for some time; as the distinction between hot and lucid, is nothing else but the memory both of a heating, and of an enlightening object.

9. The phantasms of men that sleep, are *dreams*. Concerning which we are taught by experience these five things. First, that for the most part there is neither order nor coherence in them. Secondly, that we dream of nothing but what is compounded and made up of the phantasms of sense past. Thirdly, that sometimes they proceed, as in those that are drowsy, from the interruption of their phantasms by little and little, broken and altered through sleepiness; and sometimes also they begin in the midst of sleep. Fourthly, that they

are clearer than the imaginations of waking men, except such as are made by sense itself, to which they are equal in clearness. Fifthly, that when we dream, we admire neither the places nor the looks of the things that appear to us. Now from what hath been said, it is not hard to show what may be the causes of these phenomena. For as for the first, seeing all order and coherence proceeds from frequent looking back to the end, that is, from consultation; it must needs be, that seeing in sleep we lose all thought of the end, our phantasms succeed one another, not in that order which tends to any end, but as it happeneth, and in such manner, as objects present themselves to our eyes when we look indifferently upon all things before us, and see them, not because we would see them, but because we do not shut our eyes; for then they appear to us without any order at all. The second proceeds from this, that in the silence of sense there is no new motion from the objects, and therefore no new phantasm, unless we call that new, which is compounded of old ones, as a chimera, a golden mountain, and the like. As for the third, why a dream is sometimes as it were the continuation of sense, made up of broken phantasms, as in men distempered with sickness, the reason is manifestly this, that in some of the organs sense remains, and in others it faileth. But how some phantasms may be revived, when all the exterior organs are benumbed with sleep, is not so easily shown. Nevertheless that, which hath already been said, contains the reason of this also. For whatsoever strikes the *pia mater*, reviveth some of those phantasms that are still in motion in the brain; and when any internal motion of the heart reacheth that membrane, then the predominant motion in the brain makes the phantasm. Now the motions of the heart are appetites and aversions, of which I shall presently speak further. And as appetites and aversions are generated by phantasms, so reciprocally phantasms are generated by appetites and aversions. For example, heat in the heart proceeds from anger and fighting; and again, from heat in the heart, whatsoever be the cause of it, is generated anger and the image of an enemy, in sleep. And as love and beauty stir up heat in certain organs; so heat in the same organs, from whatsoever it proceeds, often causeth desire and the image of an unresisting beauty. Lastly, cold doth in the same manner generate fear in those that sleep, and causeth them to dream of ghosts, and to have phantasms of horror and danger; as fear also causeth cold in those that wake. So reciprocal are the motions of the heart and brain. The fourth, namely, that the things we seem to see and feel in sleep, are as clear as in sense itself, proceeds from two causes; one, that having then no sense of things without us, that internal motion which makes the phantasm, in the absence of all other impressions, is predominant; and the other, that the parts of our phantasms which are decayed and worn out by time, are made up with other fictitious parts. To conclude, when we dream, we do not wonder at strange places and the appearances of things unknown to us, because admiration requires that the things appearing be new and unusual, which can happen to none but those that remember former appearances; whereas in sleep, all things appear as present.

But it is here to be observed, that certain dreams, especially such as some men have when they are between sleeping and waking, and such as happen to those that have no knowledge of the nature of dreams and are withal superstitious, were not heretofore nor are now accounted dreams. For the apparitions men thought they saw, and the voices they thought they heard in sleep, were not believed to be phantasms, but things subsisting of themselves, and objects without those that dreamed. For to some men, as well sleeping as waking, but especially to guilty men, and in the night, and in hallowed places, fear alone, helped a little with the stories of such apparitions, hath raised in their minds terrible phantasms, which have been and are still deceitfully received for things really true, under the names of *ghosts* and *incorporeal substances.*

10. In most living creatures there are observed five kinds of senses, which are distinguished by their organs, and by their different kinds of phantasms; namely, *sight, hearing, smell, taste,* and *touch;* and these have their organs partly peculiar to each of them severally, and partly common to them all. The organ of sight is partly animate, and partly inanimate. The inanimate parts are the three humours; namely, the watery humour, which by the interposition of the membrane called uvea, the perforation whereof is called the apple of the eye, is contained on one side by the first concave superficies of the eye, and on the other side by the ciliary processes, and the coat of the crystalline humor; the crystalline, which, hanging in the midst between the ciliary processes, and being almost of spherical figure, and of a thick consistence, is enclosed on all sides with its own transparent coat; and the vitreous or glassy humour, which filleth all the rest of the cavity of the eye, and is somewhat thicker than the watery humour, but thinner than the crystalline. The animate part of the organ is, first, the membrane *choroeides,* which is a part of the *pia mater,* saving that it is covered with a coat derived from the marrow of the optic

nerve, which is called the *retina;* and this *choroeides,* seeing it is part of the *pia mater,* is continued to the beginning of the *medulla spinalis* within the scull, in which all the nerves which are within the head have their roots. Wherefore all the animal spirits that the nerves receive, enter into them there; for it is not imaginable that they can enter into them anywhere else. Seeing therefore sense is nothing else but the action of objects propagated to the furthest part of the organ; and seeing also that animal spirits are nothing but vital spirits purified by the heart, and carried from it by the arteries; it follows necessarily, that the action is derived from the heart by some of the arteries to the roots of the nerves which are in the head, whether those arteries be the *plexus retiformis,* or whether they be other arteries which are inserted into the substance of the brain. And, therefore, those arteries are the complement or the remaining part of the whole organ of sight. And this last part is a common organ to all the senses; whereas, that which reacheth from the eye to the roots of the nerves is proper only to sight. The proper organ of hearing is the tympanum of the ear and its own nerve; from which to the heart the organ is common. So the proper organs of smell and taste are nervous membranes, in the palate and tongue for the taste, and in the nostrils for the smell; and from the roots of those nerves to the heart all is common. Lastly, the proper organ of touch are nerves and membranes dispersed through the whole body; which membranes are derived from the root of the nerves. And all things else belonging alike to all the senses seem to be administered by the arteries, and not by the nerves.

The proper phantasm of sight is light; and under

this name of light, colour also, which is nothing but perturbed light, is comprehended. Wherefore the phantasm of a lucid body is light; and of a coloured body colour. But the object of sight, properly so called, is neither light nor colour, but the body itself which is lucid, or enlightened, or coloured. For light and colour, being phantasms of the sentient, cannot be accidents of the object. Which is manifest enough from this, that visible things appear oftentimes in places in which we know assuredly they are not, and that in different places they are of different colours, and may at one and the same time appear in divers places. Motion, rest, magnitude, and figure, are common both to the sight and touch; and the whole appearance together of figure, and light or colour, is by the Greeks commonly called εἶδος, and εἴδωλον, and ἰδέα; and by the Latins *species* and *imago*; all which names signify no more but appearance.

The phantasm which is made by hearing, is sound; by smell, odour; by taste, savour; and by touch, hardness and softness, heat and cold, wetness, oiliness, and many more, which are easier to be distinguished by sense than words. Smoothness, roughness, rarity, and density, refer to figure, and are therefore common both to touch and sight. And as for the objects of hearing, smell, taste, and touch, they are not sound, odour, savour, hardness, &c., but the bodies themselves from which sound, odour, savour, hardness, &c. proceed; of the causes of which, and of the manner how they are produced, I shall speak hereafter.

But these phantasms, though they be effects in the sentient, as subject, produced by objects working upon the organs; yet there are also other effects besides these, produced by the same objects in the same organs;

namely, certain motions proceeding from sense, which are called *animal motions*. For seeing in all sense of external things there is mutual action and reaction, that is, two endeavours opposing one another, it is manifest that the motion of both of them together will be continued every way, especially to the confines of both the bodies. And when this happens in the internal organ, the endeavour outwards will proceed in a solid angle, which will be greater, and consequently the idea greater, than it would have been if the impression had been weaker.

11. From hence the natural cause is manifest, first, why those things seem to be greater, which, *cæteris paribus,* are seen in a greater angle: secondly, why in a serene cold night, when the moon doth not shine, more of the fixed stars appear than at another time. For their action is less hindered by the serenity of the air, and not obscured by the greater light of the moon, which is then absent; and the cold, making the air more pressing, helpeth or strengtheneth the action if the stars upon our eyes; in so much as stars may then be seen which are seen at no other time. And this may suffice to be said in general concerning sense made by the reaction of the organ. For, as for the place of the image, the deceptions of sight, and other things of which we have experience in ourselves by sense, seeing they depend for the most part upon the fabric itself of the eye of man, I shall speak of them then when I come to speak of man.

12. But there is another kind of sense, of which I will say something in this place, namely, the sense of pleasure and pain, proceeding not from the reaction of the heart outwards, but from continual action from the outermost part of the organ towards the heart. For

the original of life being in the heart, that motion in the sentient, which is propagated to the heart, must necessarily make some alteration or diversion of vital motion, namely, by quickening or slackening, helping or hindering the same. Now when it helpeth, it is pleasure; and when it hindereth, it is pain, trouble, grief, &c. And as phantasms seem to be without, by reason of the endeavour outwards, so pleasure and pain, by reason of the endeavour of the organ inwards, seem to be within; namely, there where the first cause of the pleasure or pain is; as when the pain proceeds from a wound, we think the pain and the wound are both in the same place.

Now vital motion is the motion of the blood, perpetually circulating (as hath been shown from many infallible signs and marks by Doctor Harvey, the first observer of it) in the veins and arteries. Which motion, when it is hindered by some other motion made by the action of sensible objects, may be restored again either by bending or setting strait the parts of the body; which is done when the spirits are carried now into these, now into other nerves, till the pain, as far as is possible, be quite taken away. But if vital motion be helped by motion made by sense, then the parts of the organ will be disposed to guide the spirits in such manner as conduceth most to the preservation and augmentation of that motion, by the help of the nerves. And in animal motion this is the very first endeavour, and found even in the embryo; which while it is in the womb, moveth its limbs with voluntary motion, for the avoiding of whatsoever troubleth it, or for the pursuing of what pleaseth it. And this first endeavour, when it tends towards such things as are known by experience to be pleasant, is called *appetite,* that is, an approaching; and when it shuns what is troublesome, *aversion*, or flying from it. And little infants, at the beginning and as soon as they are born, have appetite to very few things, as also they avoid very few, by reason of their want of experience and memory; and therefore they have not so great a variety of animal motion as we see in those that are more grown. For it is not possible, without such knowledge as is derived from sense, that is, without experience and memory, to know what will prove pleasant or hurtful; only there is some place for conjecture from the looks or aspects of things. And hence it is, that though they do not know what may do them good or harm, yet sometimes they approach and sometimes retire from the same thing, as their doubt prompts them. But afterwards, by accustoming themselves by little and little, they come to know readily what is to be pursued and what to be avoided; and also to have a ready use of their nerves and other organs, in the pursuing and avoiding of good and bad. Wherefore appetite and aversion are the first endeavours of animal motion.

Consequent to this first endeavour, is the impulsion into the nerves and retraction again of animal spirits, of which it is necessary there be some receptacle or place near the original of the nerves; and this motion or endeavour is followed by a swelling and relaxation of the muscles; and lastly, these are followed by contraction and extension of the limbs, which is animal motion.

13. The considerations of appetites and aversions are divers. For seeing living creatures have sometimes appetite and sometimes aversion to the same thing, as they think it will either be for their good or their hurt; while that vicissitude of appetites and aversions remains

in them, they have that series of thoughts which is called *deliberation;* which lasteth as long as they have it in their power to obtain that which pleaseth, or to avoid that which displeaseth them. Appetite, therefore, and aversion are simply so called as long as they follow not deliberation. But if deliberation have gone before, then the last act of it, if it be appetite, is called *will;* if aversion, *unwillingness.* So that the same thing is called both will and appetite; but the consideration of them, namely, before and after deliberation, is divers. Nor is that which is done within a man whilst he willeth any thing, different from that which is done in other living creatures, whilst, deliberation having preceded, they have appetite.

Neither is the freedom of willing or not willing, greater in man, than in other living creatures. For where there is appetite, the entire cause of appetite hath preceded; and, consequently, the act of appetite could not choose but follow, that is, hath of necessity followed (as is shown in chapter IX, article 5). And therefore such a liberty as is free from necessity, is not to be found in the will either of men or beasts. But if by liberty we understand the faculty or power, not of willing, but of doing what they will, then certainly that liberty is to be allowed to both, and both may equally have it, whensoever it is to be had.

Again, when appetite and aversion do with celerity succeed one another, the whole series made by them hath its name sometimes from one, sometimes from the other. For the same deliberation, whilst it inclines sometimes to one, sometimes to the other, is from appetite called *hope,* and from aversion, *fear.* For where there is no hope, it is not to be called fear, but *hate;* and where no fear, not hope, but *desire.* To conclude, all the passions, called passions of the mind, consist of appetite and aversion, except pure pleasure and pain, which are a certain fruition of good or evil; as anger is aversion from some imminent evil, but such as is joined with appetite of avoiding that evil by force. But because the passions and perturbations of the mind are innumerable, and many of them not to be discerned in any creatures besides men; I will speak of them more at large in that section which is concerning *man.* As for those objects, if there be any such, which do not at all stir the mind, we are said to contemn them.

And thus much of sense in general. In the next place I shall speak of sensible objects.

CHAPTER XXVI.

OF THE WORLD AND OF THE STARS.

1. The magnitude and duration of the world, inscrutable.—2. No place in the world empty.—3. The arguments of Lucretius for vacuum, invalid.—4. Other arguments for the establishing of vacuum, invalid.—5. Six suppositions for the solving of the phenomena of nature.—6. Possible causes of the motions annual and diurnal; and of the apparent direction, station, and retrogradation of the planets.—7. The supposition of simple motion, why likely.—8. The cause of the eccentricity of the annual motion of the earth.—9. The cause why the moon hath always one and the same face turned towards the earth.—10. The cause of the tides of the ocean.—11. The cause of the precession of the equinoxes.

CHAPTER XXVII.

OF LIGHT, HEAT, AND OF COLOURS.

1. Of the immense magnitude of some bodies, and the unspeakable littleness of others.—2. Of the cause of the light of

the sun.—3. How light heateth.—4. The generation of fire from the sun.—5. The generation of fire from collision. 6. The cause of light in glow-worms, rotten wood, and the Bolognan stone.—7. The cause of light in the concussion of sea water.—8. The cause of flame, sparks, and colliquation. 9. The cause why wet hay sometimes burns of its own accord; also the cause of lightning.—10. The cause of the force of gunpowder; and what is to be ascribed to the coals, what to the brimstone, and what to the nitre.—11. How heat is caused by attrition.—12. The distinction of light into first, second, &c.—13. The causes of the colours we see in looking through a prisma of glass, namely, of red, yellow, blue, and violet colour.—14. Why the moon and the stars appear redder in the horizon than in the midst of the heaven.—15. The cause of whiteness.—16. The cause of blackness.

1. BESIDES the stars, of which I have spoken in the last chapter, whatsoever other bodies there be in the world, they may be all comprehended under the name of intersidereal bodies. And these I have already supposed to be either the most fluid æther, or such bodies whose parts have some degree of cohesion. Now, these differ from one another in their several *consistencies, magnitudes, motions,* and *figures.* In consistency, I suppose some bodies to be harder, others softer through all the several degrees of *tenacity.* In magnitude, some to be greater, others less, and many unspeakably little. For we must remember that, by the understanding, quantity is divisible into divisibles perpetually. And therefore, if a man could do as much with his hands as he can with his understanding, he would be able to take from any given magnitude a part which should be less than any other magnitude given. But the Omnipotent Creator of the world can actually from a part of any thing take another part, as far as we by our understanding can conceive the same to be

divisible. Wherefore there is no impossible smallness of bodies. And what hinders but that we may think this likely? For we know there are some living creatures so small that we can scarce see their whole bodies. Yet even these have their young ones; their little veins and other vessels, and their eyes so small as that no microscope can make them visible. So that we cannot suppose any magnitude so little, but that our very supposition is actually exceeded by nature. Besides, there are now such microscopes commonly made, that the things we see with them appear a hundred thousand times bigger than they would do if we looked upon them with our bare eyes. Nor is there any doubt but that by augmenting the power of these microscopes (for it may be augmented as long as neither matter nor the hands of workmen are wanting) every one of those hundred thousandth parts might yet appear a hundred thousand times greater than they did before. Neither is the smallness of some bodies to be more admired than the vast greatness of others. For it belongs to the same Infinite Power, as well to augment infinitely as infinitely to diminish. To make the great orb, namely, that whose radius reacheth from the earth to the sun, but as a point in respect of the distance between the sun and the fixed stars; and, on the contrary, to make a body so little, as to be in the same proportion less than any other visible body, proceeds equally from one and the same Author of Nature. But this of the immense distance of the fixed stars, which for a long time was accounted an incredible thing, is now believed by almost all the learned. Why then should not that other, of the smallness of some bodies, become credible at some time or other? For the Majesty of God appears no less in small things than in great; and as it exceedeth human sense in the immense greatness of the universe, so also it doth in the smallness of the parts thereof. Nor are the first elements of compositions, nor the first beginnings of actions, nor the first moments of times more credible, than that which is now believed of the vast distance of the fixed stars.

Some things are acknowledged by mortal men to be very great, though finite, as seeing them to be such. They acknowledge also that some things, which they do not see, may be of infinite magnitude. But they are not presently nor without great study persuaded, that there is any mean between infinite and the greatest of those things which either they see or imagine. Nevertheless, when after meditation and contemplation many things which we wondered at before are now grown more familiar to us, we then believe them, and transfer our admiration from the creatures to the Creator. But how little soever some bodies may be, yet I will not suppose their quantity to be less than is requisite for the solving of the phenomena. And in like manner I shall suppose their motion, namely, their velocity and slowness, and the variety of their figures, to be only such as the explication of their natural causes requires. And lastly, I suppose, that the parts of the pure æther, as if it were the first matter, have no motion at all but what they receive from bodies which float in them, and are not themselves fluid.

2. Having laid these grounds, let us come to speak of causes; and in the first place let us inquire what may be the cause of the light of the sun. Seeing, therefore, the body of the sun doth by its simple circular motion thrust away the ambient ethereal substance sometimes one way sometimes another, so that those parts, which are next the sun, being moved by it, do

propagate that motion to the next remote parts, and these to the next, and so on continually; it must needs be that, notwithstanding any distance, the foremost part of the eye will at last be pressed; and by the pressure of that part, the motion will be propagated to the innermost part of the organ of sight, namely, to the heart; and from the reaction of the heart, there will proceed an endeavour back by the same way, ending in the endeavour outwards of the coat of the eye, called the *retina*. But this endeavour outwards, as has been defined in chapter xxv, is the thing which is called light, or the phantasm of a lucid body. For it is by reason of this phantasm that an object is called lucid. Wherefore we have a possible cause of the light of the sun; which I undertook to find.

3. The generation of the light of the sun is accompanied with the generation of heat. Now every man knows what heat is in himself, by feeling it when he grows hot; but what it is in other things, he knows only by ratiocination. For it is one thing to grow hot, and another thing to heat or make hot. And therefore though we perceive that the fire or the sun heateth, yet we do not perceive that it is itself hot. That other living creatures, whilst they make other things hot, are hot themselves, we infer by reasoning from the like sense in ourselves. But this is not a necessary inference. For though it may truly be said of living creatures, that *they heat, therefore they are themselves hot;* yet it cannot from hence be truly inferred that *fire heateth, therefore it is itself hot;* no more than this, *fire causeth pain, therefore it is itself in pain.* Wherefore, that is only and properly called hot, which when we feel we are necessarily hot.

Now when we grow hot, we find that our spirits

and blood, and whatsoever is fluid within us, is called out from the internal to the external parts of our bodies, more or less, according to the degree of the heat; and that our skin swelleth. He, therefore, that can give a possible cause of this evocation and swelling, and such as agrees with the rest of the phenomena of heat, may be thought to have given the cause of the heat of the sun.

It hath been shown, in the 5th article of chapter XXI, that the fluid medium, which we call the air, is so moved by the simple circular motion of the sun, as that all its parts, even the least, do perpetually change places with one another; which change of places is that which there I called fermentation. From this fermentation of the air, I have, in the 8th article of the last chapter, demonstrated that the water may be drawn up into the clouds.

And I shall now show that the fluid parts may, in like manner, by the same fermentation, be drawn out from the internal to the external parts of our bodies. For seeing that wheresoever the fluid medium is contiguous to the body of any living creature, there the parts of that medium are, by perpetual change of place, separated from one another; the contiguous parts of the living creature must, of necessity, endeavour to enter into the spaces of the separated parts. For otherwise those parts, supposing there is no vacuum, would have no place to go into. And therefore that, which is most fluid and separable in the parts of the living creature which are contiguous to the medium, will go first out; and into the place thereof will succeed such other parts as can most easily transpire through the pores of the skin. And from hence it is necessary that the rest of the parts, which are not separated, must altogether be moved outwards, for the keeping of all places full. But this motion outwards of all parts together must, of necessity, press those parts of the ambient air which are ready to leave their places, and therefore all the parts of the body, endeavouring at once that way, make the body swell. Wherefore a possible cause is given of heat from the sun; which was to be done.

* * * * * * * * *

CHAPTER XXVIII.

OF COLD, WIND, HARD, ICE, RESTITUTION OF BODIES BENT, DIAPHONOUS, LIGHTNING AND THUNDER; AND OF THE HEADS OF RIVERS.

1. Why breath from the same mouth sometimes heats and sometimes cools.—2. Wind, and the inconstancy of winds, whence.—3. Why there is a constant, though not a great wind, from east to west, near the equator.—4. What is the effect of air pent in between the clouds.—5. No change from soft to hard, but by motion.—6. What is the cause of cold near the poles.—7. The cause of ice; and why the cold is more remiss in rainy than in clear weather. Why water doth not freeze in deep wells as it doth near the superficies of the earth. Why ice is not so heavy as water; and why wine is not so easily frozen as water.—8. Another cause of hardness from the fuller contact of atoms; also, how hard things are broken.—9. A third cause of hardness from heat. 10. A fourth cause of hardness from the motion of atoms enclosed in a narrow space.—11. How hard things are softened.—12. Whence proceed the spontaneous restitution of things bent.—13. Diaphanous and opacous, what they are, and whence.—14. The cause of lightning and thunder—15. Whence it proceeds that clouds can fall again after they are once elevated and frozen.—16. How it could be that the moon was eclipsed, when she was not diametrically opposite

to the sun.—17. By what means many sums may appear at once.—18. Of the heads of rivers.

CHAPTER XXIX.

OF SOUND, ODOUR, SAVOUR, AND TOUCH.

1. The definition of sound, and the distinctions of sounds. 2. The cause of the degrees of sounds.—3. The difference between sounds acute and grave.—4. The difference between clear and hoarse sounds, whence.—5. The sound of thunder and of a gun, whence it proceeds.—6. Whence it is that pipes, by blowing into them, have a clear sound.—7. Of reflected sound.—8. From whence it is that sound is uniform and lasting.—9. How sound may be helped and hindered by the wind.—10. Not only air, but other bodies how hard soever they be, convey sound.—11. The causes of grave and acute sounds, and of concent.—12. Phenomena for smelling.—13. The first organ and the generation of smelling.—14. How it is helped by heat and by wind.—15. Why such bodies are least smelt, which have least intermixture of air in them.—16. Why odorous things become more odorous by being bruised.—17. The first organ of tasting; and why some savours cause nauseousness.—18. The first organ of feeling; and how we come to the knowledge of such objects as are common to the touch and other senses.

1. SOUND *is sense generated by the action of the medium, when its motion reacheth the ear and the rest of the organs of sense.* Now, the motion of the medium is not the sound itself, but the cause of it. For the phantasm which is made in us, that is to say, the reaction of the organ, is properly that which we call *sound.*

The principal distinctions of sounds are these; first, that one sound is stronger, another weaker. Secondly, that one is more grave, another more acute. Thirdly, that one is clear, another hoarse. Fourthly, that one is primary, another derivative. Fifthly, that one is uniform, another not. Sixthly, that one is more durable, another less durable. Of all which distinctions the members may be sub-distinguished into parts distinguishable almost infinitely. For the variety of sounds seems to be not much less than that of colours.

As vision, so hearing is generated by the motion of the medium, but not in the same manner. For sight is from pressure, that is, from an endeavour; in which there is no perceptible progression of any of the parts of the medium; but one part urging or thrusting on another propagateth that action successively to any distance whatsoever; whereas the motion of the medium, by which sound is made, is a stroke. For when we hear, the drum of the ear, which is the first organ of hearing, is stricken; and the drum being stricken, the *pia mater* is also shaken, and with it the arteries which are inserted into it; by which the action being propagated to the heart itself, by the reaction of the heart a phantasm is made which we call sound; and because the reaction tendeth outwards, we think it is without.

2. And seeing the effects produced by motion are greater or less, not only when the velocity is greater or less, but also when the body hath greater or less magnitude though the velocity be the same; a sound may be greater or less both these ways. And because neither the greatest nor the least magnitude or velocity can be given, it may happen that either the motion may be of so small velocity, or the body itself of so small magnitude, as to produce no sound at all; or either of them may be so great, as to take away the faculty of sense by hurting the organ.

From hence may be deduced possible causes of the

strength and weakness of sounds in the following phenomena.

The first whereof is this, that if a man speak through a trunk which hath one end applied to the mouth of the speaker, and the other to the ear of the hearer, the sound will come stronger than it would do through the open air. And the cause, not only the possible, but the certain and manifest cause is this, that the air which is moved by the first breath and carried forwards in the trunk, is not diffused as it would be in the open air, and is consequently brought to the ear almost with the same velocity with which it was first breathed out. Whereas, in the open air, the first motion diffuseth itself every way into circles, such as are made by the throwing of a stone into a standing water, where the velocity grows less and less as the undulation proceeds further and further from the beginning of its motion.

The second is this, that if the trunk be short, and the end which is applied to the mouth be wider than that which is applied to the ear, thus also the sound will be stronger than if it were made in the open air. And the cause is the same, namely, that by how much the wider end of the trunk is less distant from the beginning of the sound, by so much the less is the diffusion.

The third, that it is easier for one, that is within a chamber, to hear what is spoken without, than for him, that stands without, to hear what is spoken within. For the windows and other inlets of the moved air are as the wide end of the trunk. And for this reason some creatures seem to hear the better, because nature has bestowed upon them wide and capacious ears.

The fourth is this, that though he, which standeth upon the sea-shore, cannot hear the collision of the two nearest waves, yet nevertheless he hears the roaring of the whole sea. And the cause seems to be this, that though the several collisions move the organ, yet they are not severally great enough to cause sense; whereas nothing hinders but that all of them together may make sound.

3. That bodies when they are stricken do yield some a more grave, others a more acute sound, the cause may consist in the difference of the times in which the parts stricken and forced out of their places return to the same places again. For in some bodies, the restitution of the moved parts is quick, in others slow. And this also may be the cause, why the parts of the organ, which are moved by the medium, return to their rest again, sometimes sooner, sometimes later. Now, by how much the vibrations or the reciprocal motions of the parts are more frequent, by so much doth the whole sound made at the same time by one stroke consist of more, and consequently of smaller parts. For what is acute in sound, the same is subtle in matter; and both of them, namely acute sound and subtle matter, consist of very small parts, that of time, and this of the matter itself.

The third distinction of sounds cannot be conceived clearly enough by the names I have used of *clear* and *hoarse,* nor by any other that I know; and therefore it is needful to explain them by examples. When I say hoarse, I understand whispering and hissing, and whatsoever is like to these, by what appellation soever it be expressed. And sounds of this kind seem to be made by the force of some strong wind, raking rather than striking such hard bodies as it falls upon. On the contrary, when I use the word clear, I do not understand such a sound as may be easily and distinctly heard; for so whispers would be clear; but such as is made by somewhat that is broken, and such as is clamour, tinkling, the sound of a trumpet, &c., and to express it significantly in one word, noise. And seeing no sound is made but by the concourse of two bodies at the least, by which concourse it is necessary that there be as well reaction as action, that is to say, one motion opposite to another; it follows that according as the proportion between those two opposite motions is diversified, so the sounds which are made will be different from one another. And whensoever the proportion between them is so great, as that the motion of one of the bodies be insensible if compared with the motion of the other, then the sound will not be of the same kind; as when the wind falls very obliquely upon a hard body, or when a hard body is carried swiftly through the air; for then there is made that sound which I call a hoarse sound, in Greek σύριγμος. Therefore the breath blown with violence from the mouth makes a hissing, because in going out it rakes the superficies of the lips, whose reaction against the force of the breath is not sensible. And this is the cause why the winds have that hoarse sound. Also if two bodies, how hard soever, be rubbed together with no great pressure, they make a hoarse sound. And this hoarse sound, when it is made, as I have said, by the air raking the superficies of a hard body, seemeth to be nothing but the dividing of the air into innumerable and very small files. For the asperity of the superficies doth, by the eminences of its innumerable parts, divide or cut in pieces the air that slides upon it.

4. *Noise,* or that which I call clear sound, is made two ways; one, by two hoarse sounds made by opposite motions; the other, by collision, or by the sudden pulling asunder of two bodies, whereby their small particles are put into commotion, or being already in commotion suddenly restore themselves again; which motion, making impression upon the medium, is propagated to the organ of hearing. And seeing there is in this collision or divulsion an endeavour in the particles of one body, opposite to the endeavour of the particles of the other body, there will also be made in the organ of hearing a like opposition of endeavours, that is to say, of motions; and consequently the sound arising from thence will be made by two opposite motions, that is to say, by two opposite hoarse sounds in one and the same part of the organ. For, as I have already said, a hoarse sound supposeth the sensible motion of but one of the bodies. And this opposition of motions in the organ is the cause why two bodies make a noise, when they are either suddenly stricken against one another, or suddenly broken asunder.

* * * * * * * * *

12. For the finding out the cause of *smells,* I shall make use of the evidence of these following phenommena. First, that smelling is hindered by cold, and helped by heat. Secondly, that when the wind bloweth from the object, the smell is the stronger; and, contrarily, when it bloweth from the sentient towards the object, the weaker; both which phenomena are, by experience, manifestly found to be true in dogs, which follow the track of beasts by the scent. Thirdly, that such bodies, as are less pervious to the fluid medium, yield less smell than such as are more per-

vious; as may be seen in stones and metals, which, compared with plants and living creatures, and their parts, fruits and excretions, have very little or no smell at all. Fourthly, that such bodies, as are of their own nature odorous, become yet more odorous when they are bruised. Fifthly, that when the breath is stopped, at least in men, nothing can be smelt. Sixthly, that the sense of smelling is also taken away by the stopping of the nostrils, though the mouth be left open.

13. By the fifth and sixth phenomenon it is manifest, that the first and immediate organ of smelling is the innermost cuticle of the nostrils, and that part of it, which is below the passage common to the nostrils and the palate. For when we draw breath by the nostrils we draw it into the lungs. That breath, therefore, which conveys smells is in the way which passeth to the lungs, that is to say, in that part of the nostrils which is below the passage through which the breath goeth. For, nothing is smelt, neither beyond the passage of the breath within, nor at all without the nostrils.

And seeing that from different smells there must necessarily proceed some mutation in the organ, and all mutation is motion; it is therefore also necessary that, in smelling, the parts of the organ, that is to say of that internal cuticle and the nerves that are inserted into it, must be diversely moved by different smells. And seeing also, that it hath been demonstrated, that nothing can be moved but by a body that is already moved and contiguous; and that there is no other body contiguous to the internal membrane of the nostrils but breath, that is to say attracted air, and such little solid invisible bodies, if there be any such, as are intermingled with the air; it follows necessarily, that the cause of smelling is either the motion of that pure air or ethereal substance, or the motion of those small bodies. But this motion is an effect proceeding from the object of smell, and therefore, either the whole object itself or its several parts must necessarily be moved. Now, we know that odorous bodies make odour, though their whole bulk be not moved. Wherefore the cause of odour is the motion of the invisible parts of the odorous body. And these invisible parts do either go out of the object, or else, retaining their former situation with the rest of the parts, are moved together with them, that is to say, they have simple and invisible motion. They that say, there goes something out of the odorous body, call it an effluvium; which effluvium is either of the ethereal substance, or of the small bodies that are intermingled with it. But, that all variety of odours should proceed from the effluvia of those small bodies that are intermingled with the ethereal substance, is altogether incredible, for these considerations; first, that certain unguents, though very little in quantity, do nevertheless send forth very strong odours, not only to a great distance of place, but also for a great continuance of time, and are to be smelt in every point both of that place and time; so that the parts issued out are sufficient to fill ten thousand times more space, than the whole odorous body is able to fill; which is impossible. Secondly, that whether that issuing out be with strait or with crooked motion, if the same quantity should flow from any other odorous body with the same motion, it would follow that all odorous bodies would yield the same smell. Thirdly, that seeing those effluvia have great velocity of motion (as is manifest from this, that noisome odours proceeding from caverns are presently smelt at a great distance) it would follow, that, by reason there is nothing to hinder the passage of those effluvia to the organ, such motion alone were sufficient to cause smelling; which is not so; for we cannot smell at all, unless we draw in our breath through our nostrils. Smelling, therefore, is not caused by the effluvium of atoms; nor, for the same reason, is it caused by the effluvium of ethereal substance; for so also we should smell without the drawing in of our breath. Besides, the ethereal substance being the same in all odorous bodies, they would always affect the organ in the same manner; and, consequently, the odours of all things would be alike.

It remains, therefore, that the cause of smelling must consist in the simple motion of the parts of odorous bodies without any efflux or diminution of their whole substance. And by this motion there is propagated to the organ, by the intermediate air, the like motion, but not strong enough to excite sense of itself without the attraction of air by respiration. And this is a possible cause of smelling.

14. The cause why smelling is hindered by cold and helped by heat may be this; that heat, as hath been shown in chapter XXI, generateth simple motion; and therefore also, wheresoever it is already, there it will increase it; and the cause of smelling being increased, the smell itself will also be increased. As for the cause why the wind blowing from the object makes the smell the stronger, it is all one with that for which the attraction of air in respiration doth the same. For, he that draws in the air next to him, draws with it by succession that air in which is the

object. Now, this motion of the air is wind, and, when another wind bloweth from the object, will be increased by it.

15. That bodies which contain the least quantity of air, as stones and metals, yield less smell than plants and living creatures; the cause may be, that the motion, which causeth smelling, is a motion of the fluid parts only; which parts, if they have any motion from the hard parts in which they are contained, they communicate the same to the open air, by which it is propagated to the organ. Where, therefore, there are no fluid parts as in metals, or where the fluid parts receive no motion from the hard parts, as in stones, which are made hard by accretion, there can be no smell. And therefore also the water, whose parts have little or no motion, yieldeth no smell. But, if the same water, by seeds and the heat of the sun, be together with particles of earth raised into a plant, and be afterwards pressed out again, it will be odorous, as wine from the vine. And as water passing through plants is by the motion of the parts of those plants made an odorous liquor, so also of air, passing through the same plants whilst they are growing, are made odorous airs. And thus also it is with the juices and spirits, which are bred in living creatures.

16. That odorous bodies may be made more odorous by contrition proceeds from this, that being broken into many parts, which are all odorous, the air, which by respiration is drawn from the object towards the organ, doth in its passage touch upon all those parts, and receive their motion. Now, the air toucheth the superficies only; and a body having less superficies whilst it is whole, than all its parts together have after it is reduced to powder, it follows that the

same odorous body yieldeth less smell whilst it is whole, than it will do after it is broken into smaller parts. And thus much of smells.

17. The taste follows; whose generation hath this difference from that of the sight, hearing, and smelling, that by these we have sense of remote objects; whereas, we taste nothing but what is contiguous, and doth immediately touch either the tongue or palate, or both. From whence it is evident, that the cuticles of the tongue and palate, and the nerves inserted into them are the first organ of taste; and (because from the concussion of the parts of these, there followeth necessarily a concussion of the *pia mater*) that the action communicated to these is propagated to the brain, and from thence to the farthest organ, namely, the heart, in whose reaction consisteth the nature of sense.

Now, that savours, as well as odours, do not only move the brain but the stomach also, as is manifest by the loathings that are caused by them both; they, that consider the organ of both these senses, will not wonder at all; seeing the tongue, the palate and the nostrils, have one and the same continued cuticle, derived from the *dura mater*.

And that effluvia have nothing to do in the sense of tasting, is manifest from this, that there is no taste where the organ and the object are not contiguous.

By what variety of motions the different kinds of tastes, which are innumerable, may be distinguished, I know not. I might with others derive them from the divers figures of those atoms, of which whatsoever may be tasted consisteth; or from the diverse motions which I might, by way of supposition, attribute to those atoms; conjecturing, not without some likelihood of truth, that such things as taste sweet have their particles moved with slow circular motion, and their figures spherical; which makes them smooth and pleasing to the organ; that bitter things have circular motion, but vehement, and their figures full of angles, by which they trouble the organ; and that sour things have strait and reciprocal motion, and their figures long and small, so that they cut and wound the organ. And in like manner I might assign for the causes of other tastes such several motions and figures of atoms, as might in probability seem to be the true causes. But this would be to revolt from philosophy to divination.

18. By the *touch* we feel what bodies are cold or hot, though they be distant from us. Others, as hard, soft, rough, and smooth, we cannot feel unless they be contiguous. The organ of touch is every one of those membranes, which being continued from the *pia mater* are so diffused throughout the whole body, as that no part of it can be pressed, but the *pia mater* is pressed together with it. Whatsoever therefore presseth it, is felt as hard or soft, that is to say, as more or less hard. And as for the sense of rough, it is nothing else but innumerable perceptions of hard and hard succeeding one another by short intervals both of time and place. For we take notice of rough and smooth, as also of magnitude and figure, not only by the touch, but also by memory. For though some things are touched in one point, yet rough and smooth, like quantity and figure, are not perceived but by the flux of a point, that is to say, we have no sense of them without time; and we can have no sense of time without memory.

* * * * * * * * *

CHAPTER XXX.

OF GRAVITY.

1. A thick body doth not contain more matter, unless also more place, than a thin.—2. That the descent of heavy bodies proceeds not from their own appetite, but from some power of the earth.—3. The difference of gravities proceedeth from the difference of the impetus with which the elements, whereof heavy bodies are made, do fall upon the earth.—4. The cause of the descent of heavy bodies.—5. In what proportion the descent of heavy bodies is accelerated.—6. Why those that dive do not, when they are under water, feel the weight of the water above them.—7. The weight of a body that floateth, is equal to the weight of so much water as would fill the space, which the immersed part of the body takes up within the water.—8. If a body be lighter than water, then how big soever that body be, it may float upon any quantity of water, how little soever.—9. How water may be lifted up and forced out of a vessel by air.—10. Why a bladder is heavier when blown full of air, than when it is empty.—11. The cause of the ejection upwards of heavy bodies from a wind-gun.—12. The cause of the ascent of water in a weather-glass.—13. The cause of motion upwards in living creatures.—14. That there is in nature a kind of body heavier than air, which nevertheless is not by sense distinguishable from it.—15. Of the cause of magnetical virtue.

* * * * * * * * *

15. And thus much concerning the nature of body in general; with which I conclude this my first section of the Elements of Philosophy. In the first, second, and third parts, where the principles of ratiocination consist in our own understanding, that is to say, in the legitimate use of such words as we ourselves constitute, all the theorems, if I be not deceived, are rightly demonstrated. The fourth part

depends upon hypotheses; which unless we know them to be true, it is impossible for us to demonstrate that those causes, which I have there explicated, are the true causes of the things whose productions I have derived from them.

Nevertheless, seeing I have assumed no hypothesis, which is not both possible and easy to be comprehended; and seeing also that I have reasoned aright from those assumptions, I have withal sufficiently demonstrated that they may be the true causes; which is the end of physical contemplation. If any other man from other hypotheses shall demonstrate the same or greater things, there will be greater praise and thanks due to him than I demand for myself, provided his hypotheses be such as are conceivable. For as for those that say anything may be moved or produced by *itself*, by *species*, by *its own power*, by *substantial forms*, by *incorporeal substances*, by *instinct*, by *antiperistasis*, by *antipathy*, *sympathy*, *occult quality*, and other empty words of schoolmen, their saying so is to no purpose.

And now I proceed to the phenomena of man's body; where I shall speak of the *optics*, and of the *dispositions*, *affections*, and *manners* of men, if it shall please God to give me life, and show their causes.

THE DOCTRINE OF HOBBES CONCERNING THE UNREALITY OF CONSCIOUSNESS.

HUMAN NATURE.

CHAPTER II.

HUMAN NATURE.

CHAPTER II.

2. Definition of sense. 4. Four propositions concerning the nature of conceptions. 5. The first proved. 6. The second proved. 7, 8. The third proved. 9. The fourth proved. 10. The main deception of sense.

1. HAVING declared what I mean by the word *conception,* and other words equivalent thereunto, I come to the *conceptions* themselves, to shew their *differences,* their *causes,* and the *manner of the production,* so far as is necessary for this place.

2. Originally all *conceptions* proceed from the *action* of the thing itself, whereof it is the conception: now when the action is *present,* the conception it produceth is also called *sense;* and the thing by whose action the same is produced, is called the *object of the sense.*

3. By our several *organs* we have several *conceptions* of several qualities in the objects; for by *sight* we have a conception or image composed of *colour* and *figure,* which is all the notice and knowledge the object imparteth to us of its nature by the eye. By *hearing* we have a conception called *sound,* which is all the knowledge we have of the quality of the object from the ear. And so the rest of the senses are also conceptions of several qualities, or natures of their objects.

4. Because the *image* in vision consisting of *colour* and *shape* is the knowledge we have of the qualities of the object of that sense; it is no hard matter for

a man to fall into this opinion, that the same *colour* and *shape* are the *very qualities themselves;* and for the same cause, that *sound* and *noise* are the *qualities of the bell,* or of the air. And this opinion hath been so long received, that the *contrary* must needs appear a great paradox; and yet the introduction of *species visible* and *intelligible* (which is necessary for the maintenance of that opinion) passing to and fro from the *object,* is *worse* than any paradox, as being a plain *impossibility.* I shall therefore endeavour to make plain these points:

That the subject wherein colour and image are inherent, is *not* the *object* or thing seen.

That there is nothing *without us* (really) which we call an *image* or colour.

That the said image or colour is but an *apparition* unto us of the *motion,* agitation, or alteration, which the *object* worketh in the *brain,* or spirit, or some internal substance of the head.

That as in *vision,* so also in conceptions that arise from the *other senses,* the subject of their *inherence* is not the *object,* but the *sentient.*

5. Every man hath so much experience as to have seen the *sun* and the other visible objects by reflection in the *water* and *glasses;* and this alone is sufficient for this conclusion, that *colour* and *image* may be there where the *thing seen* is *not.* But because it may be said that notwithstanding the *image* in the water be not in the object, but a thing merely *phantastical,* yet there may be *colour* really in the thing itself: I will urge further this experience, that divers times men see directly the *same* object *double,* as *two candles* for *one,* which may happen from distemper, or otherwise without distemper if a man will, the organs being

either in their right temper, or equally distempered; the *colours* and *figures* in two such images of the same thing *cannot be inherent* therein, because the thing seen cannot be in *two places.*

One of these images therefore is *not inherent* in the object: but seeing the organs of the sight are then in equal temper or distemper, the *one* of them is no more inherent than the *other;* and consequently *neither* of them both are in the object; which is the first proposition, mentioned in the precedent number.

6. Secondly, that the image of any thing by *reflection* in a *glass* or *water* or the like, is *not* any thing *in* or *behind* the glass, or *in* or *under* the water, every man may grant to himself; which is the second proposition.

7. For the third, we are to consider, first that upon every *great agitation* or *concussion* of the *brain* (as it happeneth from a stroke, especially if the stroke be upon the eye) whereby the optic nerve suffereth any great violence, there *appeareth* before the *eyes* a certain light, which light is *nothing without,* but an apparition only, all that is real being the concussion or motion of the parts of that nerve; from which experience we may conclude, that *apparition of light is really nothing but motion* within. If therefore from *lucid bodies* there can be derived *motion,* so as to affect the optic nerve in such manner as is proper thereunto, there will follow an *image* of light somewhere in that line by which the motion was last derived to the eye; that is to say, in the object, if we look directly on it, and in the glass or water, when we look upon it in the line of reflection, which in effect is the third proposition; namely, that image and colour is but an apparition to us of that motion, agitation, or alteration which

the object worketh in the brain or spirits, or some *internal* substance in the head.

8. But that *from all lucid,* shining and illuminate bodies, there is a *motion produced* to the eye, and, through the eye, to the *optic* nerve, and so into the *brain,* by which that apparition of *light* or *colour* is affected, is not hard to prove. And first, it is evident that the *fire,* the only lucid body here upon earth, worketh by *motion* equally every way; insomuch as the motion thereof *stopped* or inclosed, it is presently *extinguished,* and no more fire. And further, that that motion, whereby the fire worketh, is *dilation,* and *contraction* of itself *alternately,* commonly called *scintillation* or glowing, is manifest also by experience. From such *motion* in the fire must needs arise a *rejection* or casting from itself of that part of the *medium* which is *contiguous* to it, whereby that part also rejecteth the *next,* and so successively one part beateth back another to the very *eye;* and in the same manner the *exterior* part of the eye presseth the *interior,* (the laws of refraction still observed). Now the interior coat of the eye is nothing else but a piece of the *optic* nerve; and therefore the motion is still continued thereby into the *brain,* and by *resistance* or reaction of the brain, is also a *rebound* into the optic nerve again; which we *not conceiving* as motion or rebound from *within,* do think it is *without,* and call it *light;* as hath been already shewed by the experience of a stroke. We have no reason to doubt, that the fountain of light, the *sun,* worketh by any other ways than the *fire,* at least in this matter. And thus all *vision* hath its original from such *motion* as is here described: for where there is no light, there is no sight; and therefore *colour* also must be the same thing with *light,* as being

the effect of the lucid bodies: their *difference* being only this, that when the light cometh *directly* from the fountain to the eye, or *indirectly* by reflection from *clean* and *polite* bodies, and such as have *not* any particular motion internal to alter it, we call it *light;* but when it cometh to the eye by reflection from *uneven, rough,* and coarse bodies, or such as are affected with internal motion of their own that may alter it, then we call it *colour;* colour and light differing only in this, that the one is *pure,* and the other *perturbed* light. By that which hath been said, not only the truth of the third proposition, but also the whole manner of producing light and colour, is apparent.

9. As colour is not inherent in the object, but an effect thereof upon us, caused by such motion in the object, as hath been described: so neither is *sound* in the thing we hear, but in ourselves. One manifest sign thereof is, that as a man may *see,* so also he may *hear double* or *treble,* by multiplication of *echoes,* which echoes are sounds as well as the original; and *not* being in one and the *same place,* cannot be *inherent* in the body that maketh them. Nothing can make any thing which is not in itself: the *clapper* hath no *sound* in it, but *motion,* and maketh motion in the internal parts of the bell; so the *bell* hath motion, and not sound, that imparteth *motion* to the *air;* and the *air* hath motion, but not sound; the *air* imparteth motion by the *ear* and *nerve* unto the *brain;* and the brain hath motion but not sound; from the *brain,* it reboundeth back into the nerves *outward,* and thence it becometh an *apparition without,* which we call *sound.* And to proceed to the *rest* of the *senses,* it is apparent enough, that the *smell* and *taste* of the *same thing,* are *not* the

same to *every man;* and therefore are not in the thing *smelt* or *tasted,* but in the men. So likewise the *heat* we feel from the fire is manifestly in *us,* and is quite *different* from the heat which is in the *fire:* for *our* heat is *pleasure* or *pain,* according as it is *great* or *moderate;* but in the *coal* there is no such thing. By this the fourth and last proposition is proved, *viz.* that as in vision, so also in conceptions that arise from *other* senses, the subject of their inherence is not in the object, but in the sentient.

10. And from hence also it followeth, that *whatsoever accidents* or qualities our senses make us think there be in the *world,* they be *not* there, but are *seeming* and *apparitions* only: the things that really *are* in the world without us, are those *motions* by which these seemings are caused. And this is the *great deception of sense,* which also is to be by sense *corrected:* for as sense telleth me, when I see *directly,* that the colour seemeth to *be* in the object; so also sense telleth me, when I see by *reflection,* that colour is not in the object.

THE DOCTRINE OF HOBBES CONCERNING THE NATURE OF SPIRIT AND OF GOD

SELECTIONS FROM LEVIATHAN.

CHAPTERS XI., XII., XXXI., XXXIV.

LEVIATHAN

PART I.

CHAPTER XI.

OF THE DIFFERENCE OF MANNERS.

* * * * * * * * *

Curiosity, or love of the knowledge of causes, draws a man from the consideration of the effect, to seek the cause; and again, the cause of that cause; till of necessity he must come to this thought at last, that there is some cause, whereof there is no former cause, but is eternal; which is it men call God. So that it is impossible to make any profound inquiry into natural causes, without being inclined thereby to believe there is one God eternal; though they cannot have any idea of him in their mind, answerable to his nature. For as a man that is born blind, hearing men talk of warming themselves by the fire, and being brought to warm himself by the same, may easily conceive, and assure himself, there is somewhat there, which men call *fire,* and is the cause of the heat he feels; but cannot imagine what it is like; nor have an idea of it in his mind, such as they have that see it: so also by the visible things in this world, and their admirable order, a man may conceive there is a cause of them, which men call God; and yet not have an idea, or image of him in his mind.

And they that make little, or no inquiry into the natural causes of things, yet from the fear that proceeds from the ignorance itself, of what it is that hath the power to do them much good or harm, are inclined to suppose, and feign unto themselves, several kinds of powers invisible; and to stand in awe of their own imaginations; and in time of distress to invoke them; as also in the time of an expected good success, to give them thanks; making the creatures of their own fancy, their gods. By which means it hath come to pass, that from the innumerable variety of fancy, men have created in the world innumerable sorts of gods. And this fear of things invisible, is the natural seed of that, which every one in himself calleth religion; and in them that worship, or fear that power otherwise than they do, superstition.

And this seed of religion, having been observed by many; some of those that have observed it, have been inclined thereby to nourish, dress, and form it into laws; and to add to it of their own invention, any opinion of the causes of future events, by which they thought they should be best able to govern others, and make unto themselves the greatest use of their powers.

CHAPTER XII.

OF RELIGION.

SEEING there are no signs, nor fruit of *religion,* but in man only; there is no cause to doubt, but that the seed of *religion,* is also only in man; and consisteth in some peculiar quality, or at least in some eminent degree thereof, not to be found in any other living creatures.

And first, it is peculiar to the nature of man, to be inquisitive into the causes of the events they see, some more, some less; but all men so much, as to be curious in the search of the causes of their own good and evil fortune.

Secondly, upon the sight of anything that hath a beginning, to think also it had a cause, which determined the same to begin, then when it did, rather than sooner or later.

Thirdly, whereas there is no other felicity of beasts, but the enjoying of their quotidian food, ease, and lusts; as having little or no foresight of the time to come, for want of observation, and memory of the order, consequence, and dependence of the things they see; man observeth how one event hath been produced by another; and remembereth in them antecedence and consequence; and when he cannot assure himself of the true causes of things, (for the causes of good and evil fortune for the most part are invisible,) he supposes causes of them, either such as his own fancy suggesteth; or trusteth the authority of other men, such as he thinks to be his friends, and wiser than himself.

The two first, make anxiety. For being assured that there be causes of all things that have arrived hitherto, or shall arrive hereafter; it is impossible for a man, who continually endeavoureth to secure himself against the evil he fears, and procure the good he desireth, not to be in a perpetual solicitude of the time to come; so that every man, especially those that are over provident, are in a state like to that of Prometheus. For as Prometheus, which interpreted, is *the prudent man,* was bound to the hill Caucasus, a place of large prospect, where, an eagle feeding on his liver, devoured in the day, as much as was repaired in the night: so that man, which looks too far before him, in the care of future time, hath his heart all the day long, gnawed on by fear of death, poverty, or other calamity; and has no repose, nor pause of his anxiety but in sleep.

This perpetual fear, always accompanying mankind in the ignorance of causes, as it were in the dark, must needs have for object something. And therefore when there is nothing to be seen, there is nothing to accuse, either of their good, or evil fortune, but some *power,* or agent *invisible:* in which sense perhaps it was, that some of the old poets said, that the gods were at first created by human fear: which spoken of the gods, that is to say, of the many gods of the Gentiles, is very true. But the acknowledging of one God, eternal, infinite, and omnipotent, may more easily be derived from the desire men have to know the causes of natural bodies, and their several virtues, and operations; than from the fear of what was to befall them in time to come. For he that from any effect he seeth come to pass, should reason to the next and immediate cause thereof, and from thence to the cause of that cause, and plunge himself profoundly in the pursuit of causes; shall at last come to this, that there must be, as even the heathen philosophers confessed, one first mover; that is, a first, and an eternal cause of all things; which is that which men mean by the name of God: and all this without thought of their fortune; the solicitude whereof, both inclines to fear, and hinders them from the search of the causes of other things; and thereby gives occasion of feigning of as many gods, as there be men that feign them.

And for the matter, or substance of the invisible agents, so fancied; they could not by natural cogitation, fall upon any other conceit, but that it was the same with that of the soul of man; and that the soul of man, was of the same substance, with that which appeareth in a dream, to one that sleepeth; or in a looking-glass, to one that is awake; which, men not knowing that such apparitions are nothing else but creatures of the fancy, think to be real, and external substances; and therefore call them ghosts; as the Latins called them *imagines,* and *umbræ;* and thought them spirits, that is, thin aerial bodies; and those invisible agents, which they feared, to be like them; save that they appear, and vanish when they please. But the opinion that such spirits were incorporeal, or immaterial, could never enter into the mind of any man by nature; because, though men may put together words of contradictory signification, as *spirit,* and *incorporeal;* yet they can never have the imagination of any thing answering to them: and therefore, men that by their own meditation, arrive to the acknowledgment of one infinite, omnipotent, and eternal God, chose rather to confess he is incomprehensible, and above their understanding, than to define his nature by *spirit incorporeal,* and then confess their definition to be unintelligible: or if they give him such a title, it is not *dogmatically,* with intention to make the divine nature understood; but *piously,* to honour him with attributes, of significations, as remote as they can from the grossness of bodies visible.

* * * *

PART II.

CHAPTER XXXI.

OF THE KINGDOM OF GOD BY NATURE.

* * * * * * * * *

The end of worship amongst men, is power. For where a man seeth another worshipped, he supposeth him powerful, and is the readier to obey him; which makes his power greater. But God has no ends: the worship we do him, proceeds from our duty, and is directed according to our capacity, by those rules of honour, that reason dictateth to be done by the weak to the more potent men, in hope of benefit, for fear of damage, or in thankfulness for good already received from them.

That we may know what worship of God is taught us by the light of nature, I will begin with his attributes. Where, first, it is manifest, we ought to attribute to him *existence*. For no man can have the will to honour that, which he thinks not to have any being.

Secondly, that those philosophers, who said the world, or the soul of the world was God, spake unworthily of him; and denied his existence. For by God, is understood the cause of the world; and to say the world is God, is to say there is no cause of it, that is, no God.

Thirdly, to say the world was not created, but

eternal, seeing that which is eternal has no cause, is to deny there is a God.

Fourthly, that they who attributing, as they think, ease to God, take from him the care of mankind; take from him his honour: for it takes away men's love, and fear of him; which is the root of honour.

Fifthly, in those things that signify greatness, and power; to say he is *finite*, is not to honour him: for it is not a sign of the will to honour God, to attribute to him less than we can; and finite, is less than we can; because to finite, it is easy to add more.

Therefore to attribute *figure* to him, is not honour; for all figure is finite:

Nor to say we conceive, and imagine, or have an *idea* of him, in our mind: for whatsoever we conceive is finite:

Nor to attribute to him *parts*, or *totality;* which are the attributes only of things finite:

Nor to say he is in this, or that *place:* for whatsoever is in place, is bounded, and finite:

Nor that he is *moved*, or *resteth:* for both these attributes ascribe to him place:

Nor that there be more Gods than one; because it implies them all finite: for there cannot be more than one infinite:

Nor to ascribe to him, (unless metaphorically, meaning not the passion but the effect,) passions that partake of grief; as *repentance, anger, mercy:* or of want; as *appetite, hope, desire;* or of any passive faculty: for passion, is power limited by somewhat else.

And therefore when we ascribe to God a *will*, it is not to be understood, as that of man, for a *rational appetite;* but as the power, by which he effecteth every thing.

Likewise when we attribute to him *sight,* and other acts of sense; as also *knowledge,* and *understanding;* which in us is nothing else, but a tumult of the mind, raised by external things that press the organical parts of man's body: for there is no such thing in God; and being things that depend on natural causes, cannot be attributed to him.

He that will attribute to God, nothing but what is warranted by natural reason, must either use such negative attributes, as *infinite, eternal, incomprehensible;* or superlatives, as *most high, most great,* and the like; or indefinite, as *good, just, holy, creator;* and in such sense as if he meant not to declare what he is, (for that were to circumscribe him within the limits of our fancy,) but how much we admire him, and how ready we would be to obey him; which is a sign of humility, and of a will to honour him as much as we can. For there is but one name to signify our conception of his nature, and that is, I AM: and but one name of his relation to us, and that is, *God;* in which is contained Father, King, and Lord.

* * * *

CHAPTER XXXIV.

OF THE SIGNIFICATION OF SPIRIT, ANGEL, AND INSPIRATION IN THE BOOKS OF HOLY SCRIPTURE.

SEEING the foundation of all true ratiocination, is the constant signification of words; which in the doctrine following, dependeth not, as in natural science, on the will of the writer, nor, as in common conversation, on vulgar use, but on the sense they carry in the

Scripture; it is necessary, before I proceed any further, to determine, out of the Bible, the meaning of such words, as by their ambiguity, may render what I am to infer upon them, obscure, or disputable. I will begin with the words BODY and SPIRIT, which in the language of the Schools are termed, *substances, corporeal,* and *incorporeal.*

The word *body,* in the most general acceptation, signifieth that which filleth, or occupieth some certain room, or imagined place; and dependeth not on the imagination, but is a real part of that we call the *universe.* For the *universe,* being the aggregate of all bodies, there is no real part thereof that is not also *body;* nor any thing properly a *body,* that is not also part of that aggregate of all *bodies,* the *universe.* The same also, because bodies are subject to change, that is to say, to variety of apparence to the sense of living creatures, is called *substance,* that is to say, *subject* to various accidents: as sometimes to be moved; sometimes to stand still; and to seem to our senses sometimes hot, sometimes cold, sometimes of one colour, smell, taste, or sound, sometimes of another. And this diversity of seeming, produced by the diversity of the operation of bodies on the organs of our sense, we attribute to alterations of the bodies that operate, and call them *accidents* of those bodies. And according to this acceptation of the word, *substance* and *body* signify the same thing; and therefore *substance incorporeal* are words, which when they are joined together, destroy one another, as if a man should say, an *incorporeal body.*

But in the sense of common people, not all the universe is called body, but only such parts thereof as they can discern by the sense of feeling, to resist their force, or by the sense of their eyes, to hinder them from a farther prospect. Therefore in the common language of men, *air*, and *aerial substances*, use not to be taken for *bodies*, but (as often as men are sensible of their effects) are called *wind*, or *breath*, or (because the same are called in the Latin *spiritus*) *spirits*; as when they call that aerial substance, which in the body of any living creature gives it life and motion, *vital* and *animal spirits*. But for those idols of the brain, which represent bodies to us, where they are not, as in a looking-glass, in a dream, or to a distempered brain waking, they are, as the apostle saith generally of all idols, nothing; nothing at all, I say, there where they seem to be; and in the brain itself, nothing but tumult, proceeding either from the action of the objects, or from the disorderly agitation of the organs of our sense. And men, that are otherwise employed, than to search into their causes, know not of themselves, what to call them; and may therefore easily be persuaded, by those whose knowledge they much reverence, some to call them *bodies*, and think them made of air compacted by a power supernatural, because the sight judges them corporeal; and some to call them *spirits*, because the sense of touch discerneth nothing in the place where they appear, to resist their fingers: so that the proper signification of *spirit* in common speech, is either a subtle, fluid, and invisible body, or a ghost, or other idol or phantasm of the imagination. But for metaphorical significations, there be many: for sometimes it is taken for disposition or inclination of the mind; as when for the disposition to controul the sayings of other men, we say, *a spirit of contradiction*; for *a disposition to uncleanness, an unclean spirit*; for *perverseness, a froward spirit*; for *sullen-*

ness, a dumb spirit; and for *inclination to godliness and God's service, the Spirit of God:* sometimes for any eminent ability or extraordinary passion, or disease of the mind, as when *great wisdom* is called *the spirit of wisdom;* and *madmen* are said to be *possessed with a spirit.*

Other signification of *spirit* I find nowhere any; and where none of these can satisfy the sense of that word in Scripture, the place falleth not under human understanding; and our faith therein consisteth not in our opinion; but in our submission; as in all places where God is said to be a *Spirit;* or whereby the *Spirit of God,* is meant God himself. For the nature of God is incomprehensible; that is to say, we understand nothing of *what he is,* but only *that he is;* and therefore the attributes we give him, are not to tell one another, *what he is,* nor to signify our opinion of his nature, but our desire to honour him with such names as we conceive most honourable amongst ourselves.

Gen. i. 2. *The Spirit of God moved upon the face of the waters.* Here if by the *Spirit of God* be meant God himself, then is *motion* attributed to God, and consequently *place,* which are intelligible only of bodies, and not of substances incorporeal; and so the place is above our understanding, that can conceive nothing moved that changes not place, or that has not dimension; and whatsoever has dimension, is body. But the meaning of those words is best understood by the like place, (*Gen.* viii. 1.) where when the earth was covered with waters, as in the beginning, God intending to abate them, and again to discover the dry land, useth the like words, *I will bring my Spirit upon the earth, and the waters shall be diminished:* in which place, by *Spirit* is understood a wind, that is an air or *spirit moved,* which might be called, as in the former place, the *Spirit of God,* because it was God's work.

* * * *

Concerning the creation of *angels,* there is nothing delivered in the Scriptures. That they are spirits, is often repeated: but by the name of spirit, is signified both in Scripture, and vulgarly, both amongst Jews and Gentiles, sometimes thin bodies: as the air, the wind, the spirits vital and animal of living creatures; and sometimes the images that rise in the fancy in dreams and visions; which are not real substances, nor last any longer than the dream, or vision they appear in; which apparitions, though no real substances, but accidents of the brain; yet when God raiseth them supernaturally, to signify his will, they are not improperly termed God's messengers, that is to say, his *angels.*

And as the Gentiles did vulgarly conceive the imagery of the brain, for things really subsistent without them, and not dependent on the fancy; and out of them framed their opinions of *demons,* good and evil; which because they seemed to subsist really, they called *substances;* and, because they could not feel them with their hands, *incorporeal:* so also the Jews, upon the same ground, without any thing in the Old Testament that constrained them thereunto, had generally an opinion, except the sect of the Sadducees, that those apparitions, which it pleased God sometimes to produce in the fancy of men, for his own service, and therefore called them his *angels,* were substances, not dependent on the fancy, but permanent creatures of God; whereof those which they thought were good to them, they esteemed the *angels of God,* and those they thought would hurt them, they called *evil angels,* or evil spirits; such as was the spirit of Python, and the spirits of madmen, of lunatics and epileptics: for they esteemed such as were troubled with such diseases, *demoniacs.*

But if we consider the places of the Old Testament where angels are mentioned, we shall find, that in most of them, there can nothing else be understood by the word *angel,* but some image raised, supernaturally, in the fancy, to signify the presence of God in the execution of some supernatural work; and therefore in the rest, where their nature is not expressed, it may be understood in the same manner.

* * * *

To mention all the places of the Old Testament where the name of angel is found, would be too long. Therefore to comprehend them all at once, I say, there is no text in that part of the Old Testament, which the Church of England holdeth for canonical, from which we can conclude, there is, or hath been created, any permanent thing, understood by the name of *spirit* or *angel,* that hath not quantity; and that may not be by the understanding divided; that is to say, considered by parts; so as one part may be in one place, and the next part in the next place to it; and, in sum, which is not (taking body for that, which is somewhat or some where,) corporeal; but in every place, the sense will bear the interpretation of angel, for messenger; as John Baptist is called an angel, and Christ the Angel of the Covenant; and as, according to the same analogy, the dove and the fiery tongues, in that they were signs of God's special presence, might also be called angels. Though we find in *Daniel* two names of angels, Gabriel and Michael; yet it is clear out of the text itself, (*Dan.* xii. 1) that by Michael is meant Christ, not as an angel, but as a prince: and that Gabriel, as the like apparitions made to other holy men in their sleep, was nothing but a supernatural phantasm, by which it seemed to Daniel, in his dream, that two saints being in talk, one of them said to the other, *Gabriel, Let us make this man understand his vision:* for God needeth not to distinguish his celestial servants by names, which are useful only to the short memories of mortals. Nor in the New Testament is there any place, out of which it can be proved, that angels, except when they are put for such men as God hath made the messengers and ministers of his word or works, are things permanent, and withal incorporeal. That they are permanent, may be gathered from the words of our Saviour himself, (*Matt.* xxv. 41) where he saith, it shall be said to the wicked in the last day, *Go ye cursed into everlasting fire prepared for the Devil and his angels:* which place is manifest for the permanence of evil angels, (unless we might think the name of Devil and his angels may be understood of the Church's adversaries and their ministers); but then it is repugnant to their immateriality; because everlasting fire is no punishment to impatible substances, such as are all things incorporeal. Angels therefore are not thence proved to be incorporeal. In like manner where St. Paul says, (1 *Cor.* vi. 3) *Know ye not that we shall judge the angels?* and 2 *Pet.* ii. 4, *For if God spared not the angels that sinned, but cast them down into hell:* and (*Jude* i. 6) *And the angels that kept not their first estate, but left their own habitation, he hath reserved in everlasting chains under darkness unto the judgment of the last day:* though it prove the permanence of angelical nature, it confirmeth also their materiality. And (*Matt.* xxii. 30) *In the resurrection men do neither marry nor give in marriage, but are as the angels of God in heaven:* but in the resurrection men shall be permanent, and not incorporeal; so therefore also are the angels.

There be divers other places out of which may be drawn the like conclusion. To men that understand the signification of these words, *substance,* and *incorporeal;* as *incorporeal* is taken, not for subtle body, but for *not body;* they imply a contradiction: insomuch as to say, an angel or spirit is in that sense an incorporeal substance, is to say in effect, there is no angel nor spirit at all. Considering therefore the signification of the word *angel* in the Old Testament, and the nature of dreams and visions that happen to men by the ordinary way of nature; I was inclined to this opinion, that angels were nothing but supernatural apparitions of the fancy, raised by the special and extraordinary operation of God, thereby to make his presence and commandments known to mankind, and chiefly to his own people. But the many places of the New Testament, and our Saviour's own words, and in such texts, wherein is no suspicion of corruption of the Scripture, have extorted from my feeble reason, an acknowledgment and belief, that there be also angels substantial, and permanent. But to believe they be in no place, that is to say, no where, that is to say, nothing, as they, though indirectly, say, that will have them incorporeal, cannot by Scripture be evinced.

SELECTED PASSAGES

FROM

ELEMENTORUM PHILOSOPHIÆ SECTIO PRIMA DE CORPORE.

SELECTIONS FROM DE CORPORE.

The *Elements of Philosophy Concerning Body* is an English version, by an unnamed translator, of the *De Corpore* of Hobbes. Though the translation was revised by Hobbes, it is none the less an unsatisfactory version — sometimes inexact, again so literal that it is fairly uncouth, and at times even positively misleading. The following selections, topically ordered, comprise definitions and statements of fundamental importance to the system of Hobbes. It will appear that the Latin is both clearer and more forcible than the corresponding English; yet the English rendering of these passages will be found to be "for substance of doctrine" correct.

I. IMAGINARY SPACE AND TIME.

CHAPTER VII. (1), (2) AND (3), IN PART.

1. Doctrinæ naturalis exordium, optime (ut supra ostensum est) a privatione, id est, a ficta universi sublatione, capiemus. Supposita autem tali rerum annihilatione, quæret fortasse aliquis, quid reliquum esset, de quo homo aliquis (quem ab hoc universo rerum interitu unicum excipimus) philosophari, vel omnino ratiocinari, vel cui rei nomen aliquod ratiocinandi causa imponere posset.

Dico igitur, remansuras illi homini, mundi et corporum omnium, quæ, ante sublationem eorum, oculis aspexerat, vel aliis sensibus perceperat, ideas, id est memoriam imaginationemque magnitudinum, motuum, sonorum, colorum, &c. atque etiam eorum ordinis et partium; quæ omnia etsi ideæ tantum et phantasmata sint, ipsi imaginanti interne accidentia, nihilominus tanquam externa, et a virtute animi minime dependentia, apparitura esse. . . .

2. Jam si meminerimus, seu phantasma habuerimus alicujus rei, quæ extiterat ante suppositam rerum externarum sublationem, nec considerare velimus, qualis ea res erat,* sed simpliciter quod erat extra animum, habemus id, quod appellamus *spatium,* imaginarium quidem, quia merum phantasma, sed tamen illud ipsum, quod ab omnibus sic appellatur. . . . Reversus itaque ad institutum, spatii definitionem hanc esse dico,

* Cf. the English version.

*spatium est phantasma rei existentis, quatenus existentis,** id est, nullo alio ejus rei accidente considerato præterquam quod apparet extra imaginantem.

3. . . . Tota ergo definitio temporis talis est, *tempus est phantasma motus, quatenus in motu imaginamur prius et posterius, sive successionem;** quæ convenit cum definitione Aristotelica, *tempus est numerus motus secundum prius* et *posterius* et *tempus est phantasma motus numerati,* illud autem *tempus est mensura motus* non ita recte dicitur, nam tempus per motum, non autem motum per tempus, mensuramus.

II. BODY AND ACCIDENT.

a. Definitions.

Chapter VIII. (1) and (2), in part.

1. Intellecto jam quid sit spatium imaginarium, in quo nihil esse externum supposuimus, sed meram eorum, quæ olim existentia imagines suas in animo reliquerant, privationem; supponamus deinceps aliquid eorum rursus reponi, sive creari denuo; necesse ergo est ut creatum illud sive repositum, non modo occupet aliquam dicti spatii partem, sive cum ea coincidat et coextendatur, sed etiam esse aliquid, quod ab imaginatione† nostra non dependet. Hoc autem ipsum est quod appellari solet, propter extensionem quidem, *corpus;* propter independentiam autem a nostra cogitatione† *subsistens per se;* et propterea quod extra nos

* Cf. the English.

† Cf. the English, and note both how loosely it conforms to the Latin and how it fails to distinguish these similar but differentiated terms.

subsistit, *existens;* denique quia sub spatio imaginario substerni et supponi videtur* ut non sensibus sed ratione tantum aliquid ibi esse intelligatur, *suppositum* et *subjectum.* Itaque definitio corporis hujusmodi est, *corpus est quicquid non dependens a nostra cogitatione cum spatii parte aliqua coincidit vel coextenditur.*

2. Quid autem sit accidens non tam facile definitione quam exemplis explicari potest. . . . His ut satisfiat, optime, . . . respondent illi qui accidens definiunt esse *modum corporis, juxta quem*† *concipitur;* quod est idem ac si dicerent, *accidens esse facultatem corporis qua sui conceptum nobis imprimit.*

b. Body as occupying real space.

Chapter VIII. (4).

4. Extensio corporis idem est quod magnitudo ejus, sive id quod aliqui vocant *spatium reale;* magnitudo autem illa non dependet a cogitatione nostra, sicut spatium imaginarium, hoc enim illius effectus est, magnitudo causa; hoc animi, illa corporis extra animum existentis accidens est.

III. MOTION.

a. Definitions.

Chapter XV. (1), first sentence.

Proxima ordine tractatio est de *motu* et *magnitudine,* corporum accidentibus maxime communibus.

* Cf. the English.
† Cf. the English.

Chapter VIII. (10), in part.

Motus est continua unius loci relictio et alterius acquisitio; locus autem, qui relinquitur, terminus a quo, qui acquiritur, terminus ad quem dici solet; continuam dico, propterea quod corpus quantulumcumque sit, non potest totum simul a toto loco priore ita excedere, ut pars ejus non sit in parte quæ sit utrique loco, nimirum relicto et acquisito, communis. . . .

Moveri autem aliquid nisi in tempore concipi non potest. Est enim tempus, ex definitione, phantasma, id est, conceptus motus; itaque concipere moveri aliquid non in tempore esset concipere motum non concepto motu, quod est impossible.

b. Cause of Motion.

Chapter IX. (7) in part.

Causa motus, nulla esse potest in corpore nisi contiguo et moto. Sint enim duo corpora quælibet non contigua, inter quæ aut spatium, quod interjacet, vacuum sit, aut si plenum, plenum tamen corpore quiescente, propositorum autem corporum unum quiescere supponatur. Dico quieturum semper; nam si movebitur; causa ejus motus per caput 8, articulum 19, erit in corpore* externo; si igitur, inter ipsum et externum illud, vacuum spatium sit, possumus concipere, utcunque se habeant corpora externa vel ipsum patiens (modo supponatur nunc quiescere), quieturum esse quamdiu ab iis* non contingitur; cum autem causa (per definitionem) sit aggregatum accidentium om-

* Cf. the English.

nium quibus suppositis effectum non sequi concipi non potest, accidentia quæ sunt vel in externis vel in ipso patiente, causa futuri motus non *erit*, similiter quia concipi potest id quod jam quiescit quieturum adhuc, etiamsi ab alio corpore contingatur modo corpus illud non moveatur, non erit causa motus in contiguo corpore quiescente. Itaque causa motus in corpore nulla est, nisi in contiguo et moto.

c. All Change is Motion.

Chapter IX. (9).

Hoc posito, necesse est ut mutatio aliud non sit præter partium corporis mutati motum. Primo enim mutari nihil dicimus præterquam quod sensibus nostris aliter apparet quam ante apparuit. Secundo, illæ apparentiæ sunt ambæ effectus producti in sentiente; itaque si diversi sunt, necesse est per præcedentem, ut vel agentis pars aliqua ante quiescens jam moveatur, et sic mutatio consistit in eo motu; vel ante mota, nunc aliter moveatur, et sic quoque consistit mutatio in novo motu, vel ante mota nunc quiescat, quod fieri nisi per motum non posse supra demonstravimus, et ita rursus mutatio motus est, vel denique aliquid horum contingit patienti vel parti ejus, atque ita omni modo mutatio consistet in motu partium ejus corporis quod sentitur, vel ipsius sentientis, vel utriusque. Itaque mutatio *motus* est (nimirum partium agentis vel patientis) quod erat propositum demonstrare. Huic autem consequens est, quietem nullius rei causam esse, neque omnino per eam quicquam *agi*, ut quæ neque motus neque mutationis ullius causa sit.

Catalogue of Publications
of the
Open Court Publishing Company
Chicago, Monon Building, 324 Dearborn St.
London, Kegan Paul, Trench, Trübner & Co., Ltd.

SUNDARA ROW, T.

GEOMETRIC EXERCISES IN PAPER-FOLDING.
With Half-Tones from Photographs of Exercises. Pages, x + 148
Cloth, $1.00 net (4s. 6d. net).

COPE, E. D.

THE PRIMARY FACTORS OF ORGANIC EVOLUTION.
121 cuts. Pp. xvi, 547. Cloth, $2.00 net (10s.).

MÜLLER, F. MAX.

THREE INTRODUCTORY LECTURES ON THE SCIENCE OF THOUGHT.
128 pages. Cloth, 75c (3s. 6d).

THREE LECTURES ON THE SCIENCE OF LANGUAGE.
112 pages. 2nd Edition. Cloth, 75c (3s. 6d.).

ROMANES, GEORGE JOHN.

DARWIN AND AFTER DARWIN.
Three Vols., $4.00. Singly, as follows:
1. The Darwinian Theory. 46 pages. 125 illustrations. Cloth, $2.00
2. Post-Darwinian Questions. Heredity and Utility. Pp. 338. $1.50
3. Post-Darwinian Questions. Isolation and Physiological Selection Pp. 181. $1.00.

AN EXAMINATION OF WEISMANNISM.
236 pages. Cloth, $1.00 net.

THOUGHTS ON RELIGION.
Third Edition, Pages, 184. Cloth, gilt top, $1.25 net.

A CANDID EXAMINATION OF THEISM.
Pages, xi., 197. Cloth, $2.00.

SHUTE, D. KERFOOT.

FIRST BOOK IN ORGANIC EVOLUTION.
9 colored plates, 39 cuts. Pp. xvi + 285. Price, $2.00 net (7s. 6d. net).

CUMONT, FRANZ.

THE MYSTERIES OF MITHRA.
Pages, xii., 230. $1.50 net (7s. 6d. net).

HILBERT, DAVID,

THE FOUNDATIONS OF GEOMETRY.
With many new editions still unpublished in German. Translated by E. J. Townsend. Pp. 140. Price, $1.00 net (4s. 6d. net).

LAGRANGE, JOSEPH LOUIS.

LECTURES ON ELEMENTARY MATHEMATICS.
With portrait of the author. Pp. 172. Price, $1 00 net (4s. 6d. net).

CARUS, PAUL.

THE HISTORY OF THE DEVIL, AND THE IDEA OF EVIL.
311 Illustrations. Pages, 500. Price, $6 00 (30s.).

THE CROWN OF THORNS.
A Story of the Time of Christ. Illustrated. Pages, 73. Cloth, 75c net (3s. 6d. net).

EROS AND PSYCHE.
Illustrations by Paul Thumann. Pp. 125. Cl., $1.50 net (6s. net).

WHENCE AND WHITHER?
196 pages. Cloth, 75c net (3s. 6d. net).

THE ETHICAL PROBLEM.
Second edition, revised and enlarged. 351 pages. Cloth, $1.25 (6s. 6d.).

FUNDAMENTAL PROBLEMS.
Third edition. 372 pp. Cl., $1.50 (7s. 6d.).

HOMILIES OF SCIENCE.
317 pages. Cloth, Gilt Top, $1.50 (7s. 6d.).

THE IDEA OF GOD
Fourth edition. 32 pages. Paper 15c (9d.).

THE SOUL OF MAN.
2nd ed. 182 cuts. 482 pages. Cloth, $1.50 net (6s. net).

THE CHIEF'S DAUGHTER.
Illustrated. Pp. 54. Cloth, $1.00 net (4s. 6d. net).

THE RELIGION OF SCIENCE.
Second, extra edition. Pp. 103. Cloth, 50c net (2s. 6d.).

PRIMER OF PHILOSOPHY
240 pages. Third Edition. Cloth, $1.00 (5s.).

THE GOSPEL OF BUDDHA. According to Old Records.
Seventh Edition. Pp. 275. Cloth, $1.00 (5s.). In German, $1.25 (6s. 6d.)

BUDDHISM AND ITS CHRISTIAN CRITICS.
Pages, 311. Cloth, $1 25 (6s. 6d.).

KARMA. A STORY OF EARLY BUDDHISM.
Illustrated by Japanese artists. Crêpe paper, 75c (3s. 6d.).

NIRVANA: A STORY OF BUDDHIST PSYCHOLOGY.
American edition. 60c net (3s. net).

LAO-TZE'S TAO TEH KING.
Chinese-English. Pp. 360. Cloth, $3.00 (15s.).

GOETHE AND SCHILLER'S XENIONS.
Pages, vii., 162. $1.00 (4s. 6d.)

DAS EVANGELIUM BUDDHAS.
Pages, 352. $1.25.

GODWARD.
50c (2s. 6d.).

SACRED TUNES FOR THE CONSECRATION OF LIFE.
50c (2s. 6d.).

OUR NEED OF PHILOSOPHY.
Pages, 14. Paper, 5c (3d.).

SCIENCE A RELIGIOUS REVELATION.
Pages, 21. Paper, 5c (3d.).

TRUTH IN FICTION.
$1 00 (4s. 6d.).

THE AGE OF CHRIST.
Pages, 34. Paper, 15c (9d.).

THE SURD OF METAPHYSICS.
Pages, vii., 233. Cloth, $1.25 net (6s. 6d. net).

MILLS, LAWRENCE H.

THE GATHAS OF ZARATHUSHTRA (ZOROASTER) IN METRE AND RHYTHM.
Pages, 196. $2.00.

FINK, KARL.

A BRIEF HISTORY OF MATHEMATICS.
From the German. Pp, 333. Cloth, $1.50 net (5s. 6d. net).

SCHUBERT, HERMANN.

MATHEMATICAL ESSAYS AND RECREATIONS.
Pp. 149. Cuts, 37. Cloth, 75c net (3s. net).

HUC AND GABET, MM.

TRAVELS IN TARTARY, THIBET AND CHINA.
100 cuts. Pp. 688. 2 vols. $2.00 (10s.). One vol., $1.25 net (5s. net).

CORNILL, CARL HEINRICH.

THE PROPHETS OF ISRAEL.
Pp., 200. Cloth, $1.00 net (5s.).

HISTORY OF THE PEOPLE OF ISRAEL.
Pp. vi + 325. Cloth, $1 50 (7s. 6d.).

GESCHICHTE DES VOLKES ISRAEL.
Pages, 330. $2.00 (7s. 6d.).

THE RISE OF THE PEOPLE OF ISRAEL.
50c (2s. 6d.).

POWELL, J. W.

TRUTH AND ERROR; or, the Science of Intellection.
Pp. 423. Cloth, $1.75 (7s. 6d.).

BUDGE, E. A. W.

BOOK OF THE DEAD.
420 vignettes. 3 vols. Cloth, $3.75 net.

A HISTORY OF EGYPT.
8 volumes. $10.00.

HUTCHINSON, WOODS.

THE GOSPEL ACCORDING TO DARWIN.
Pp. xii + 241. Price, $1.50 (6s.).

AÇVAGHOSHA.

DISCOURSE ON THE AWAKENING OF FAITH in the Mahâyâna.
From the Chinese. Pp., 176. Cl., $1.25 net (5s. net).

HUEPPE, FERDINAND.

THE PRINCIPLES OF BACTERIOLOGY.
28 Woodcuts. Pp. x + 467. Price, $1.75 net (9s.).

RIBOT, TH.

THE PSYCHOLOGY OF ATTENTION.

THE DISEASES OF PERSONALITY.

THE DISEASES OF THE WILL.
Cloth, 75 cents each (3s. 6d.). *Full set, cloth, $1.75* (9s.).

EVOLUTION OF GENERAL IDEAS.
Pp 231. Cloth, $1.25 (5s.).

EDMUNDS, ALBERT J.

HYMNS OF THE FAITH (DHAMMAPADA).
Being an Ancient Anthology Preserved in the Short Collection of the Sacred Scriptures of the Buddhists. Pp. xiv+110. Cloth, $1 net.

DELITZSCH, F.

BABEL AND BIBLE.
Two Lectures. With Criticisms and the Author's Replies. 75c net.

HAUPT, PAUL.

BIBLICAL LOVE DITTIES.
5c (3d.).

HOLYOAKE, G. J.

ENGLISH SECULARISM, A CONFESSION OF BELIEF.
Pages, xiii., 146. 50c net.

INGRAHAM, ANDREW.

SWAIN SCHOOL LECTURES.
Pages, 200. $1.00 net (4s. 6d. net).

INOUYE, J.

SKETCHES OF TOKYO LIFE.
Pages, 108. 75c (3s. 6d.).

LEIBNITZ.

LEIBNITZ'S METAPHYSICS, ETC.
Transl. by Dr. George R. Montgomery. 75c (3s. 6d.).

MACH ERNST.

THE SCIENCE OF MECHANICS.
Transl. by T. J. McCormack. Pages, xx., 605. $2.00 net (7s. 6d. net)

THE ANALYSIS OF THE SENSATIONS.
Pages, xi., 208. $1.25 net (4s. 6d. net).

POPULAR SCIENTIFIC LECTURES.
Transl. by T. J. McCormack. Pages, 415. $1.50 net (6s. net).

PORTRAITS.

PHILOSOPHICAL PORTRAITS. 25c each. Set, $6.25.

PSYCHOLOGICAL PORTRAITS. 25c each. Set, $3.75.
Both sets on one order, $7.50.

RADAU, DR. HUGO.

THE CREATION-STORY OF GENESIS I.
Pages, 70, vi. Boards, 75c net (3s. 6d. net).

STANLEY, H.

PSYCHOLOGY FOR BEGINNERS.
Pages, 44. 40c net.

WAGNER, RICHARD.

A PILGRIMAGE TO BEETHOVEN.
Pages, vii., 40. 50c net (2s. 6d. net).

YAMADA, K.

SCENES FROM THE LIFE OF BUDDHA.
From the paintings of Keichyu Yamada. $2.50 net.

DE MORGAN, AUGUSTUS.

ON THE STUDY AND DIFFICULTIES OF MATHEMATICS.
Pp. viii+288. Cloth, $1.25 net (4s. 6d. net).

ELEMENTARY ILLUSTRATIONS OF THE DIFFERENTIAL AND INTEGRAL CALCULUS.
New reprint edition. Price, $1.00 net (4s. 6d. net).

FREYTAG, GUSTAV.

THE LOST MANUSCRIPT. A Novel.
2 vols. 953 pages. Extra cloth, $4.00 (21s). One vol., cl., $1.00 (5s.).

MARTIN LUTHER.
Illustrated. Pp. 130. Cloth, $1.00 net (5s.).

TRUMBULL, M. M.

THE FREE TRADE STRUGGLE IN ENGLAND.
Second Edition. 296 pages. Cloth, 75c (3s. 6d.).

WHEELBARROW: ARTICLES AND DISCUSSIONS ON THE LABOR QUESTION
With portrait of the author. 303 pages. Cloth, $1.00 (5s.).

GUNKEL, H.

THE LEGENDS OF GENESIS.
From the German. Pp. 164. Cloth, $1.00 net (4s. 6d. net).

OLDENBERG, H.

ANCIENT INDIA: ITS LANGUAGE AND RELIGIONS.
Pp. 110. Cloth, 50c net (2s. 6d.).

CONWAY, MONCURE D.

SOLOMON, AND SOLOMONIC LITERATURE.
Pp. 243. Cloth, $1.50 net (6s.).

DEDEKIND, R.

ESSAYS ON THE THEORY OF NUMBER.
Trans. by W. W. Beman. Pp. 115. Cl., 75 cents net (3s. net).

GARBE, RICHARD.

THE REDEMPTION OF THE BRAHMAN. A TALE OF HINDU LIFE.
Laid paper. Gilt top. 96 pages. Price, 75c (3s. 6d.).

THE PHILOSOPHY OF ANCIENT INDIA.
Pp. 89. Cloth, 50c net (2s. 6d.).

LÉVY-BRUHL, L.

HISTORY OF MODERN PHILOSOPHY IN FRANCE.
23 Portraits. Pp. 500. Cloth, $3.00 net (12s. net).

TOPINARD, PAUL.

SCIENCE AND FAITH.
Pp. 374. Cloth, $1.50 net (6s. 6d. net).

BINET, ALFRED.

THE PSYCHOLOGY OF REASONING.
Pp. 193. Cloth, 75c net (3s. 6d.).

THE PSYCHIC LIFE OF MICRO-ORGANISMS.
Pp. 135. Cloth, 75c (3s. 6d.).

N. B. Send for our large ILLUSTRATED CATALOGUE, containing full details of our publications and of our two magazines, *The Open Court* and *The Monist*.

The Religion of Science Library.

Bi-monthly reprints of standard works, philosophical classics, etc. Yearly, $1.50. Separate copies according to prices quoted.

No. 1. *The Religion of Science.* By Paul Carus. 25c (1s. 6d.).
2. *Three Introductory Lectures on the Science of Thought.* By F. Max Müller. 25c (1s. 6d.).
3. *Three Lectures on the Science of Language.* F. Max Müller 25c (1s. 6d.).
4. *The Diseases of Personality.* By Th. Ribot. 25c (1s. 6d.).
5. *The Psychology of Attention.* By Th. Ribot. 25c (1s. 6d.).
6. *The Psychic Life of Micro-Organisms.* By Alfred Binet. 25c (1s. 6d.).
7. *The Nature of the State.* By Paul Carus. 15c (9d.).
8. *On Double Consciousness.* By Alfred Binet. 15c (9d.).
9. *Fundamental Problems.* By Paul Carus. 50c (2s. 6d.).
10. *The Diseases of the Will.* By Th. Ribot. 25c (1s. 6d.).
11. *The Origin of Language.* By Ludwig Noiré. 15c (9d.).
12. *The Free Trade Struggle in England.* M. M. Trumbull. 25c (1s. 6d.)
13. *Wheelbarrow on the Labor Question.* By M. M. Trumbull. 35c (2s.)
14. *The Gospel of Buddha.* By Paul Carus. 35c (2s.).
15. *The Primer of Philosophy.* By Paul Carus. 25c (1s. 6d.).
16. *On Memory,* and *The Specific Energies of the Nervous System.* By Prof Ewald Hering. 15c (9d.).
17. *The Redemption of the Brahman.* A Novel. R. Garbe. 25c (1s. 6d.).
18. *An Examination of Weismannism.* By G. J. Romanes. 35c (2s.).
19. *On Germinal Selection.* By August Weismann. 25c (1s. 6d.).
20. *Lovers Three Thousand Years Ago.* By T. A. Goodwin. (Out of print.)
21. *Popular Scientific Lectures.* By Ernst Mach. 50c (2s. 6d.).
22. *Ancient India: Its Language and Religions.* By H. Oldenberg. 25c (1s. 6d.).
23. *The Prophets of Israel.* By Prof. C. H. Cornill. 25c (1. 6d.).
24. *Homilies of Science.* By Paul Carus. 35c (2s.).
25. *Thoughts on Religion.* By G. J. Romanes. 50c (2s. 6d.).
26. *The Philosophy of Ancient India.* By Prof. Richard Garbe. 25c (1s. 6d.)
27. *Martin Luther.* By Gustav Freytag. 25c (1s. 6d.).
28. *English Secularism.* By George Jacob Holyoake. 25c (1s. 6d.).
29. *On Orthogenesis.* By Th. Eimer. 25c (1s. 6d.).
30. *Chinese Philosophy.* By Paul Carus. 25c (1s. 6d.).
31. *The Lost Manuscript.* By Gustav Freytag. 60c (3s.).
32. *A Mechanico-Physiological Theory of Organic Evolution.* By Carl von Naegeli. 15c (9d.).
33. *Chinese Fiction.* By Dr. George T. Candlin. 15c (9d.).
34. *Mathematical Essays and Recreations.* By H. Schubert. 25c (1s. 6d.)
35. *The Ethical Problem.* By Paul Carus. 50c (2s. 6d.).
36. *Buddhism and Its Christian Critics.* By Paul Carus. 50c (2s. 6d.).
37. *Psychology for Beginners.* By Hiram M. Stanley. 20c (1s.).
38. *Discourse on Method.* By Descartes. 25c (1s. 6d.).
39. *The Dawn of a New Era.* By Paul Carus. 15c (9d.)
40. *Kant and Spencer.* By Paul Carus. 20c (1s.).
41. *The Soul of Man.* By Paul Carus. 75c (3s. 6d.).
42. *World's Congress Addresses.* By C. C. Bonney. 15c (9d.).
43. *The Gospel According to Darwin.* By Woods Hutchinson. 50c (2s. 6d.).
44. *Whence and Whither.* By Paul Carus. 25c (1s. 6d.).
45. *Enquiry Concerning Human Understanding.* By David Hume. 25c (1s. 6d.).
46. *Enquiry Concerning the Principles of Morals.* By David Hume, 25c (1s. 6d.).
47. *The Psychology of Reasoning.* By Alfred Binet. 25c (1s. 6d.).
48. *The Principles of Human Knowledge.* By George Berkeley. 25c (1s. 6d.).
49. *Three Dialogues Between Hylas and Philonous.* By George Berkeley. 25c (1s. 6d.).
50. *Public Worship: A Study in the Psychology of Religion.* By John P. Hylan. 25c (1s. 6d.).
51. *Descartes' Meditations, with Selections from the Principles.* 35c (2s.).
52. *Leibniz's Metaphysics, Correspondence, and Monadology.* 50c (2s.).
53. *Kant's Prolegomena.* 50c (2s. 6d.).
54. *Anselm's Proslogium, Monologium, and Cur Deus Homo.* 50c (2s. 6d.).
55. *The Canon of Reason and Virtue.* By Dr. Paul Carus. 25c (1s. 6d.).